Assessment in Educational Therapy

Assessment in Educational Therapy offers essential grounding, skills, and ethical approaches for understanding and conducting assessments in the context of educational therapy. Six clear, straightforward chapters guide graduate students and trainees of the field to use scores, observation, and hypothesis testing to create strengths-based assessments and intervention strategies that can be delivered orally or in written reports. The book is the first to describe and critique all the standardized assessment instruments that qualified educational therapists can use to measure skills in reading, written expression, mathematics, and processing. Real-world case studies, practical takeaways of key concepts, resources for self-study, reflective questions, and other readers' tools enliven this comprehensive yet accessible reference.

Marion Marshall, MS, BCET, FAET, is a Board-Certified Educational Therapist and Emerita Professor at Holy Names University, USA, where she was Director of the Educational Therapy Program and Clinical Director of the Raskob Learning Institute.

Assessment in Educational Therapy

Marion Marshall

First published 2020
by Routledge
52 Vanderbilt Avenue, New York, NY 10017

and by Routledge
2 Park Square, Milton Park, Abingdon, Oxon OX14 4RN

Routledge is an imprint of the Taylor & Francis Group, an informa business

© 2020 Taylor & Francis

The right of Marion Marshall to be identified as author of this work has been asserted by her in accordance with sections 77 and 78 of the Copyright, Designs and Patents Act 1988.

All rights reserved. No part of this book may be reprinted or reproduced or utilized in any form or by any electronic, mechanical, or other means, now known or hereafter invented, including photocopying and recording, or in any information storage or retrieval system, without permission in writing from the publishers.

Trademark notice: Product or corporate names may be trademarks or registered trademarks, and are used only for identification and explanation without intent to infringe.

Library of Congress Cataloging-in-Publication Data
A catalog record for this title has been requested

ISBN: 978-0-367-36288-1 (hbk)
ISBN: 978-0-367-40720-9 (pbk)
ISBN: 978-0-367-80869-3 (ebk)

Typeset in Galliard
by Taylor & Francis Books

Printed in the United Kingdom
by Henry Ling Limited

Contents

List of illustrations	viii
Acknowledgements	ix

1 Introduction and Assessment in the Context of Educational Therapy 1

The Foundation 1
Is There a Difference Between a Test and an Assessment? 4
Assessment in the Context of Educational Therapy 4
Assessment during a Session 5
Types of Assessment Instruments 6
Screening Tools 7
Standards-based Instruments 7
Informal Measures 7
Summary 8
Self-review Questions for Students and Professionals 8
Questions for Parents 9

2 Ethics and Foundational Practices in Administering Standardized Assessments 10

Ethics 10
Foundational Practices in Administering Standardized
  Assessments 14
Which Standardized Assessments Measure Reading, Written
  Expression, Mathematics and Processing Skills? 15
Test Format and the Learner's Profile 32

vi   *Contents*

3   The Basics of Psychometrics Explained   45

Introduction 45
Avoid Common Errors 46
Should I Use Age or Grade Equivalent Scores? 49
About Percentile Ranks 50
Standard Deviation 51
How Test Scores Are Derived 52
Z-scores 55
Interpreting the Scores 55
Standard Error of Measurement 56
Confidence Level or Confidence Intervals 57
Reminders 59
Summary 59
Self-review Questions for Students and Professionals 59
Questions for Parents 60

4   Creating the Student's Profile   62

Introduction 62
What if there is No Problem? 62
Asking Questions to Create a Working Hypothesis 64
Constellations 64
Contributions of Non-Standardized Instruments 67
Using Standards-Based, Criterion Reference Tests and Rubrics 68
Link Hypothesis Testing with Observations and the Student's
  Spontaneous Remarks 69
The Context of Assessment 73
Examining Assessment Results to Create the Student's Profile 75
An Approach to Analyzing Assessment Scores 77
Self-review questions for students and professionals 79

5   Writing a High-Quality Assessment Report   81

Introduction 81
Establish a Purpose 81
Know the Audience 82
Determine the Findings 83
Avoid Professional Jargon 84
Focus on the Individual, not the Scores 84
Write a Strengths-based Report 86
Synthesize Information in a Clear, Organized, and
  Analytical Manner 86

Contents vii

Write in a Professional Voice 88
The Nature of Recommendations 90
Conclusion 96
Self-review Questions for Students and Professionals 96
Questions for Parents 96

6   How to Orally Present Your Findings   99

Preparing to Present 99
Beginning the Meeting 103
Presenting the Results Visually 104
The Summary and Recommendations 108
Conclusion 109
Self-review Questions for Students and Professionals 110
Questions for Parents 111

Index   112

Illustrations

Figures

3.1	Assessment Cascade	47
3.2	The Bell-shaped Curve	53
3.3	Normal Distribution SAT Scores	54
3.4	SEM Confidence Band	58
4.1	Hypothesis Testing	66
4.2	Interaction Triangle	70
6.1	Horizontal Scale Scores (Sample)	105
6.2	Cassie's Scores Vertical Scale	107

Tables

2.1	Examiner's Qualifications	13
2.2	Quick Reference to Reading Assessments	38
2.3	Quick Reference to Written Expression Assessments	40
2.4	Quick Reference to Mathematics Assessments	42
2.5	Quick Reference to Processing Assessments	44
3.1	Commonly Used Terms in Standardized Assessment	49
4.1	Cassie's WJ-IV-ACH and Key Math-3 Scores	76
4.2	Cassie's Strengths, Weaknesses, and Questions	78

Acknowledgements

I would like to personally thank all of those who have been important in my professional life. Thank you to all the special educators in Antioch Unified School District who encouraged my beginnings in the field. A special thank you goes to all the independent school administrators who supported my work: Dr. Leo Gaspardone, Sheila Puckett, Abby Guinn, and Katherine Dinh. Thanks to all of those professional colleagues who gave rise to this book: Dr. Charles Ahern whose years of insightful conversations improved my practice; Dianne Matthaei, who co-authored two articles with me and graciously allowed me to use some of that content here. In giving me permission, Dianne wrote, "This book needs to be written, and I think you are the best person to write it!" Thanks to those colleagues who thoughtfully inquired, "How is the book going, Marion?" Thank you Jane Adelizzi, whose encouragement last summer was supportive. Dorothy Ungerleider, who is a "living legend" and role model for all Educational Therapists, viewed my assessment webinar and said, "You have to write this book!" Thanks to Ann Kaganoff, who has shared her thoughtful approach to educational therapy at conferences and in her recent book, *Best Practices in Educational Therapy*. Ann "planted the seed," provided the impetus and on-going encouragement for writing this book. She introduced me to Daniel Schwartz, Education Editor, at Routledge. I am deeply grateful to you both for the inspiration and opportunity.

Thank you to all the families who allowed me to assess their child, and to all the students whose heartfelt comments have enriched my work and understanding. Thank you to the current and past Holy Names University Librarians who safeguard the assessment instruments and provide excellent support for the faculty and students at HNU. I am indebted to all the educational therapy graduate students who helped me further and refine my understanding of assessment by being a part of each assessment class for the past 15 years.

Importantly, I am grateful for Patrick who taught me profound lessons about being a parent. When was the last time you heard your child say, "I'm proud of you, Mom"? Thank you, Chelsea. Lastly, thank you to Geoff Underwood, who continuously offered loving support, patiently read each

x   *Acknowledgements*

chapter multiple times, posed insightful questions or proposed suggestions for improvements. Much credit goes to him for his encouragement for all my new endeavors and my happiness.

Thank you, all.

1 Introduction and Assessment in the Context of Educational Therapy

The Foundation

This chapter creates the foundation for thinking about assessment as it applies to educational therapists (ETs). I use the term "student" since my work has primarily been with elementary-aged children. If you work with a differently-aged population, substitute *client* as you read. I use the term "parents" generically. Please substitute *guardian* in your reading, if applicable. Myer et al. stated that:

> Although tests can assist clinicians with case formulation and treatment recommendations, they are only tools. Tools do not think for themselves. Like a stethoscope, a blood pressure gauge, or an MRI scan, a test is a dumb tool—and the worth of the tool cannot be separated from the sophistication of the clinician who draws inferences from it and then communicates with clients and other professionals.
>
> (Quoted in Schrank & Flanagan 2003: 126)

When I teach a graduate-level class in advanced assessment, I always ask small groups, "Why does one assess?" in the first class session. Typically, all are thinking of the initial, standardized assessments. Those who are training as special education teachers confer together and have their answers very quickly. Murmurs can be heard among that group, "What is taking *them* so long?" as the educational therapist candidates discuss and ponder the question.

From the special education teachers' perspective there are only three reasons to assess: to determine eligibility for special education services, to measure whether annual Individualized Educational Plan (IEP) goals have been met, and to determine if the student remains qualified for services at the triannual review.

When a list of the class responses is written on the white board for all to view, ten to fifteen reasons emerge from the educational therapist candidates, beyond determining eligibility. Recently, the list included:

- Ascertaining actual skill levels.
- Establishing objective data about skills.
- Informing parents about "what is going on."

2 Introduction

- Identifying academic strengths and weaknesses in a variety of areas.
- As a means for understanding a complex student's learning profile.
- Giving information that would allow parents to advocate for their child.
- Providing age-appropriate information that could allow a student to advocate for her/himself.
- Offering objective information that might empower the child and reduce stigma.
- Observing how a student perseveres through the challenging aspects of the tests.
- Individualizing future learning strategies.
- Identifying the need for accommodations and modifications.
- Helping the classroom teacher(s) understand and support the student better.
- Bonding with the student.

As the board fills with these responses, the *murmuring* from the special education teacher candidates becomes audible and full of disbelief, "*No one does all that!*"

Because ETs generally do not assess cognitive skills and, therefore, do not "determine eligibility," especially in terms of the discrepancy model, assessment serves vastly different purposes and the types of assessment used may vary greatly from the standardized, formal assessment used in the public schools. Since public schools assess to determine eligibility for services, a qualifying, eligibility category "label" is required. Generally, ETs do not diagnose and, therefore do not apply a qualifying term. Rather, educational therapists *describe*.

There are many advantages to describing instead of diagnosing:

1 A qualifying "label," such as a Specific Learning Disability, may reduce a student's complex learning profile in an overly narrow way which may mask the overlapping and/or compounding learning issues.
2 A qualifying term is *never* strengths-based. It only emphasizes "what's wrong," which may lessen the family's understanding for the need to take action.
3 A qualifying label may feel like a "death sentence" instead of providing a helpful and a more hopeful explanation. For example, dyscalculia is not an inherently descriptive term. A thoughtful description may lead to greater self-awareness. "Oh! I'm not dumb! I have *good* math problem solving skills but struggle with computation. If I really try to memorize those math facts ..."

Meet "Cassie" in Chapters 3–6 to see how each aspect of assessment relates to her case.

So, why do ETs assess? That seems like a straightforward question, but how, when and why do ETs assess? Most agree that assessment should be

Introduction 3

purposeful. It ought to answer a set of questions. Some ETs conduct formal assessment for payment to answer referral questions. Few assess to determine eligibility for special education services. However, ETs assess regularly and at different points in working a case—to determine baseline skills of a new client, to set learning goals, to judge the learning accomplished within a session, and when reading a report from an allied professional that contains assessment data. Most ETs will do some level of assessment when preparing a written progress report—or when the report is informal and presented orally to a parent or guardian or in preparation for a meeting at the client's school. There are many different types of assessment and each serves a different purpose.

Since assessment is conducted to answer questions, explicitly determining the questions to be answered will govern what assessments will be used. Further, it will establish whether the ET is qualified to answer the referral questions or whether one needs to refer to an allied professional (see Chapter 2 regarding the *ethics* of giving assessments for the ET). A vague referral question such as "My child's teacher thinks she is behind" is neither adequate nor helpful. Nor does it give insight into whether the parent(s) have the same level of concern as the teacher.

It is critical to know *when* to start the assessment process. Often, time needs to be spent ascertaining whether the referral questions are shared by the parents also. If the primary driving force is the school or teacher(s), it is likely too soon to begin the assessment process. Conversations need to occur that will enable the parent to feel that answering questions *now* is a good idea. Or, if one parent is ready to have their student assessed, the other parent may be opposed. If the process is rushed, the *findings* may not be believed and the recommendations not carried out. I recall a father, "Ben," sitting patiently through the initial public school IEP meeting but growing obviously restive as the meeting went on. When I asked why he seemed to be uncomfortable or frustrated, he exploded with, "My son can't have anything wrong with him—he can play Tetris at Level 20!" Clearly, time should have spent helping this parent understand the teacher's view about the child's academic strengths and weakness *before* requesting and receiving written permission to conduct a formal assessment. (See Chapter 4 for strategies to develop a common understanding about the nature of the issues before you begin the assessment process.)

Since referral questions guide evaluations, it is imperative to elicit questions from all concerned parties. Different stakeholders may have different questions. Teachers and parents may have variant views. Each parent may have different concerns. Few things are more disappointing than spending hours assessing a student, scoring and analyzing the results and writing a detailed report, only to find that you failed to answer the essential question(s) because you did not identify them adequately. Early in my career as an ET, I was contacted by a mother who wished to have her 6th-grade daughter's reading skills assessed. She was worried because "Camille" seemed to "skip over" many words as she was reading aloud. I was comfortable and confident in my ability to conduct a

4   *Introduction*

reading assessment. So, dates were scheduled and a fee was determined. Camille was cooperative and rapport was established easily. When I had concluded the assessment, scored the results, analyzed the findings and written a report, I was certain that I had relevant information to share.

A part of my assessment process is to "debrief" with the student as another way of confirming the assessment results (see Chapter 4). In our conversation at the end of the final assessment session, Camille readily agreed with my findings and as I began to draw the session to a close, she asked anxiously, "When are we going to do something about math?" I was perplexed. No one had said anything about her math skills being a concern. So, when I asked, Camille erupted with, "I'm falling behind! I don't understand what my teacher is saying! I can't do the homework! I need help in *math*!" Obviously, I had failed to elicit referral questions from *all* the stakeholders.

Understanding and identifying the referral questions is essential to providing effective assessment. "Why is my 2nd-grader struggling to learn to read?" is a separate question from "Is my child dyslexic?" and, "Why does my child read so slowly?" is completely different from "Why doesn't my 5th-grader understand what she reads?" Each of those questions calls for the use of distinct assessment instruments or a separate set of measures.

Is There a Difference Between a Test and an Assessment?

In a public school setting, when a teacher says, "This student needs to be tested," it is often a cry of frustration because the teacher has reached the limit of her understanding of how to help the child learn, to pay attention, or to retain previously studied concepts. The teacher is often seeking "testing" in hopes of gaining special education services for the student. But, administering a test or tests is different than conducting assessment. Testing is usually done to measure a specific skill, at one moment in time, to determine skill level or understanding of content. A weekly spelling test is given. A vocabulary test is given in Spanish II. An algebra test measures the student's ability to solve quadratic equations. Classroom tests are useful to determine how an individual compares to the others in the group. They can be used as formative assessment to see whether the class is learning a concept, as a whole. If it is a key concept, it best not to move too quickly if the group does not demonstrate sufficient understanding. In this example, that exasperated teacher is seeking a formal assessment since she has conducted many measures of *testing* in her classroom.

Assessment in the Context of Educational Therapy

Assessment is much more than administering a set of instruments and obtaining scores. It is imperative to observe and note self-regulatory behaviors such as level of engagement, attention, sustained attention, mental energy, effort, and persistence. Also, one should note examples of strategic planning, problem-solving, and use of language. Assessment instruments, in and of themselves, are valuable

Introduction 5

tools but are not the sole answer. Your careful observations during the assessment process are essential and contribute to a better understanding of the student. Nancy Mather (quoted in Schrank & Flanagan 2003: 188) believes that "test results assist with judgment; they are not a substitute." Most recognize that when they reach for an instrument (be it standardized or informal) to document a starting place for their work, they are conducting an assessment. A skilled assessor values the student's approach to tasks, strategies, efficiency, and behaviors as much as the actual scores derived.

Assessment during a Session

The author wishes to broaden the ET's, informal, definition of assessment. Assessment can also take place *within* each session. Be a curious observer of what is happening in each session. Constructive information can be gained by watching the student's level of engagement, noting successes and recording errors to be analyzed later. Error analysis is conscientiously paying attention to the errors a student makes. It allows the ET to dig deeply into examining the patterns of strengths and weaknesses observed. Error analysis is an invaluable tool for the educational therapist. A single non-repeated error is not of great importance. Likely, the student is becoming fatigued or temporarily lost focus on the task. However, when a student creates a number of errors it is best to note them for analysis. Are they different types of errors? Is there a pattern to the errors? Is the repeated error a product of incomplete learning, a misconception, or partial learning applied too broadly? (Often the case in math.) For example:

1. The student adds the denominator in a fraction problem rather than finding the common denominator. [2/3 + 1/4 = 3/7]
2. When reading aloud, the student disregards the ending punctuation which changes the meaning of some sentences.
3. The student does not "double the final consonant" when adding a suffix to a word whose base contains a "short vowel." [plan becomes planed instead of planned]

Thoughtful analysis may inform the ET about an instructional approach to address the error(s). Often, the reason for the error is not immediately discernable. In that case, hypothesis testing may produce the answer. Ask yourself, "What variable can I change in my instruction to see if the error disappears?" "What questions can I ask to hear what the student's approach is?" Asking the student to "think aloud" while working can be another useful tool. "Pretend I am your friend who was absent yesterday. How did your teacher tell the class to solve this problem?" *Task analysis* within each session is extremely valuable. Think about the task itself and the underlying requirements in performing the task. How much understanding of language is involved? How many steps does the task require? How much working memory is needed? What other cognitive and academic skills are necessary? Think about

6 Introduction

what you know (and are learning about) the student's cognitive profile. Where can the student leverage her strengths? How often does the task play into his area(s) of weaknesses? How strategic is her approach? Has he integrated past experiences or do you need to remind him to utilize the strategies previously demonstrated? Conduct regular dialogue with your students about their approach to each task and ask about how they are experiencing learning itself.

Ask yourself reflective questions such as "What's working? Where is the breakdown point? How can I structure the next session to address those breakdown points? How can I vary the task or teaching prompt to examine what is working and what is not?" This careful examination should be used to determine needed adjustments and the focus for the next session(s). Noticing fatigue, avoidance, the approaches to tasks and level of persistence displayed between activities *within a session* is imperative to designing effective future sessions.

One learns to pay attention to whether the *pace* within a session matches the client's profile. Am I speaking too fast? Is my language too complex? Can the student decode the words in isolation but not in the context of reading a text? Since every session contains many types of activities, am I changing types of tasks too frequently or am I requiring the student to labor on one part of a lesson too long?

Similarly, think about whether the number of practice items is sufficient for learning. Or, does the *numerosity* become overwhelming and, therefore, not actually support learning? Notice how many math problems are done correctly and if there a point where errors creep into later problems. Note how many words (or paragraphs) the student can read accurately before miscues occur. Careful observation of the work *within a session* and *patterns from session to session* is a valuable form of assessment whose benefits cannot be overstated.

Types of Assessment Instruments

Some educational therapists use an *assessment battery* to measure a student's strengths, weaknesses, processing skills and approaches to tasks. Formal assessments are those that are *standardized*, normed and produce a Standard Score and Percentile Rank which compares that student's performance to age- or grade-level peers. (See Chapter 3 for a discussion about using age- and grade-level equivalents in scoring.) A *battery* is the term for a group of assessments used in combination to answer the referral questions and to determine academic and processing strengths and weaknesses.

Many ETs use a variety of standardized and non-standardized measures in their assessment battery. School reports, past assessment results, developmental history, and relevant medical history will be reviewed. Teachers and parents/guardians will be asked about how the student presents at school and at home. Rating scales may be used. Observations will be made during the assessment process. A student's spontaneous comments will be noted. Some ETs also observe the student in their school setting as a part of the assessment process.

Introduction 7

Screening Tools

One may assess using a screening instrument to "rule in" or "rule out" some factor/aspect that may be affecting learning. Some measures are standardized and others are not. The benefits of using a *screening instrument* is that it may provide a shortcut to finding the information you seek. These type of measures may *also* be used to identify student strengths and to locate misconceptions. These tools tend to be limited in their scope and are relatively easy to administer and score. However, by narrowing the question(s) being asked, one may overlook information about other relevant questions you did not think to ask. And, if you are not using multiple measures, you will not be able to create a thorough view of a student's *pattern* of strengths and issues.

Standards-based Instruments

Some very useful assessments are *standards-based*. The similarity of name with standardized measures can be confusing. Generally, these assessments are not normed but are designed to specifically align and reflect state grade-level curricular standards and expectations. The standards-based assessments used by ETs are most often those in the areas of math and reading. See *The Glossary of Education Reform* at www.edglossary.org/standards-based

Criterion-Reference Tests (also known as Diagnostic Tests)

These tools are designed to discretely measure what skills a student has already mastered. A *criterion-reference test* or *diagnostic test* is useful in determining what skills a student knows in the areas of mathematics, phonics, reading, and spelling. Each provides quick diagnostic information about what skills the student currently has acquired and where "gaps" in knowledge exist. These types of assessments "look backwards rather than forwards. It assesses what the learner already knows and/or the nature of difficulties that the learner might have ..." *Principles of Assessment* (University of Exeter n.d.) as cited in *Teaching Quality Assurance & Enhancement*. These types of measures are very useful since they allow the ET to immediately ascertain where to intervene and which skills to teach next. Additionally, they can help establish baseline data.

Informal Measures

These assessment tools can be published or self-made. Although *informal measures* are rarely normed, the ETs who use them regularly claim they obtain such useful data that few other measures are needed. Self-made assessments are often developed to provide *specific* information. The ET becomes very skilled at the administration, scoring and analysis of the results. Administration can be more fluid and readily adjusted without invalidating the results. Often, there is less reliance on the test scores and greater focus on the learner's process and

8   *Introduction*

approach. This may afford more opportunities to interact while observing the "style" of the learner and place more emphasis on information gathering as a way to establish goals for a treatment plan. This author posits that these assessments almost become "normed" for the examiner since s/he knows what are typical answers for their client base, what are efficient approaches to the tasks, and what are atypical or anomalous responses and approaches. Many ETs have developed what Kaganoff (2019: 35) describes as "diagnostic tasks" which are "characterized by important critical attributes" to assess core competencies that allow one to develop an intervention plan and gauge progress over time. However, not using *any* standardized instruments may overlook the breadth and the benefits of these instruments provide by setting this current client's scores against a rigorously normed group. The ET's self-made test is subjective. A normed assessment instrument is objective and measures against a group much larger than the ET's client base.

Summary

Assessment is an ongoing process for the ET. It should answer important questions. Work to specify and refine the referral questions. One will assesses using different tools to answer varying questions. Tools can be combined to serve your purpose(s). Carefully establishing the questions to be answered will enable the ET to determine if s/he is qualified to provide the answers. Assessment is an *integrative process* which attempts to create a holistic view of the student and does not measure a single skill. A well-designed and properly conducted assessment can provide valid and valuable information for the educational therapist. Because it is *descriptive*, it can create greater self-understanding and self-advocacy for the client. Assessment allows one to effectively establish treatment goals, prioritize instructional needs, and select appropriate methodologies. A quality assessment enhances communication between "stakeholders"—the client, parents or guardians, and school personnel (Marshall & Matthaei 2013). Assessment is a continuous process for the ET that need not necessarily mean using an assessment instrument. Observation, task analysis, error analysis and monitoring the student's approach to learning *within* and *between* sessions are also valuable forms of assessment.

Self-review Questions for Students and Professionals

1   What questions can you ask to define the scope of the parent/guardian's referral question(s)?
2   What referral question(s) are beyond your training?
3   If the questions(s) are beyond the scope of your training, do you have the names of allied professionals to make a referral?
4   What specific standardized assessments might you use to answer the following different referral questions? (See Chapter 2 for descriptions of standardized tests.)

    a   Why is my 2nd-grader struggling to learn to read?

b   Is my child dyslexic?
c   Why does my child read so slowly?
d   Why doesn't my 5th-grader understand what she reads?

Questions for Parents

1   Is there a difference between testing and assessment?
2   What types of assessments are usually given your child?
3   Did a recent assessment answer your *specific* questions?
4   If not, could you prepare those questions and submit them in advance next time?
5   Who performs the "ongoing" assessment that contains valuable information regarding your student's learning?
6   If you are the assessor, do you need help learning how to monitor progress on a more incremental basis? Where could you get that help?

Resources

Ahern, C.A. & de Kirby, K. (2011). *Beyond Individual Differences Organizing Processes, Information Overload, and Classroom Practices.* New York: Springer.

Alfonso, V.C & Flanagan, D.P. (2018). *Essentials of KTEA-3 and WIAT-III Assessment.* Hoboken, NJ: John Wiley & Sons.

Kimbell, A.-M. & Dilworth Gabel, A. (2018) Ethics of Technology and Clinician Responsibility. Retrieved from https://nationalpsychologist.com/2018/03/ethics-of-technology-and-clinician-responsibility/104292.html

Marshall, M. (2013). Beyond the Scores: Examining the Context and Purpose of Assessment. *The Educational Therapist,* 34: 9–25.

Mather, N. (1993). *Critical Issues in the Diagnosis of Learning Disabilities Addressed by the Woodcock–Johnson Psychoeducational Battery-Revised.* Brandon, VT: Clinical Psychology Publishing Co.

Mather, N. & Wendling, B. (2003). Instructional Implications from the Woodcock–Johnson III. In F.A. Schrank & D.F. Flanagan (Eds.), *WJ III Clinical Use and Interpretation: Scientist Practitioner Perspectives* (pp. 93–124). New York: Academic Press.

Schneider, J.W., Lichenberger, E.O., Mather, N. & Kaufman, N. (2018). *Essentials of Assessment Report Writing.* Hoboken, NJ: John Wiley & Sons.

References

Kaganoff, A. (2019). *Best Practices in Educational Therapy.* New York: Routledge.

Marshall, M. & Matthaei, D. (2013). Guidelines for Conducting Standardized Assessment. *The Educational Therapist,* 34(1): 27–28.

Schrank, F. & Flanagan, D. eds. (2003). *WJ III Clinical Use and Interpretation Science-Practitioner Perspectives.* San Diego, CA: Academic Press.

University of Exeter (n.d.) Teaching Quality Assurance and Enhancement: Principles of Assessment Definition of Criterion Referenced Tests. Retrieved from https://as.exeter.ac.uk/tqae/academicdevelopment/assessmentandfeedback/principlesofassessment/typesofassessment-definitions

2 Ethics and Foundational Practices in Administering Standardized Assessments

Ethics

Every professional organization has a Code of Ethics. Professionals need to know what it contains, abide by the code, and practice accordingly. A code of ethics directs internal and external behaviors. The Association of Educational Therapists (AET) code of ethics was adopted by AET Executive Committee in February, 1985, reissued in October 1997, again in August 1999 and most recently in March 2015. The *Code of Ethics and Standards for the Professional Practice of Educational Therapy* (Association of Educational Therapists 2016) was developed through an adaptation of the code of ethics and standards for professional practice of the Council for Exceptional Children (CEC). Permission was granted by CEC for the adaptation. Pertinent to this book is the part of the code which states that an educational therapist (ET) is "skilled in formal and informal educational assessment, synthesis of information from other specialists and from parents, and in the development and implementation of appropriate remedial programs for school-related learning and behavior problems" (Association of Educational Therapists 2016).

Two of the relevant guiding principles are: "Educational Therapists shall be committed to the development of professional skills appropriate to the special needs of clients, and devoid of false claims or guarantees" and "Educational Therapists provide only those professional services for which they have been adequately trained." Other related principles in the code of ethics state that educational therapists strive to:

A. Develop and interpret individual goals and objectives for educational therapy, based upon appropriate assessment procedures and/or local school mandates, in cooperation with client and parents.

B. Select and use appropriate assessment instruments, recognizing their limitations with respect to reliability, validity, and bias.

C. Use only those assessment instruments for which they have been adequately trained.

D. Seek interpretation of assessment data from professionals in related fields (e.g. medical, psychological, speech/language, neuropsychological).

Ethics and Foundational Practices 11

Educational Therapists follow both AET ethical guidelines and all applicable laws of the state(s) in which they practice.

(Association of Educational Therapists 2016)

Publishers of standardized instruments include examiner qualifications in their manuals. For example, in the Woodcock–Johnson IV Tests of Achievement (WJ-IV-ACH) *Technical Manual*: "The examiner qualifications for the WJ-IV-ACH have been informed by the joint Standards for Educational and Psychological Testing (American Educational Research Association [AERA], American Psychological Association [APA], & the National Council on Measurement in Education [NCME], 1999)" (McGrew, LaForte & Schrank 2014). Three standards are listed. The first pertains to the assessor and the second and third to the programs who train in assessment:

Standard 11.3—Responsibility for test use should be assumed by or delegated only to those individuals who have the training, professional credentials, and experience necessary to handle this responsibility.

(McGrew et al. 2014: 114)

Standard 13.10—Those responsible for educational testing programs should ensure that the individuals who administer and score the test(s) are proficient in the appropriate test administration, procedures and scoring procedures and that they understand importance of adhering to the directions provided by the test developer.

(McGrew et al. 2014: 147)

Standard 13.13—Those responsible for educational testing programs should ensure that the individuals who interpret the test results to make decisions ... are qualified to do so or are assisted by and consult with persons who are so qualified.

(McGrew et al. 2014: 148)

The manuals for comprehensive achievement assessments such as the Wechsler Individual Achievement Test, 3rd edition (WIAT-III) and the WJ-IV-ACH state that interpretation of the results require:

a level of formal education ... typically documented by successful completion of an applicable graduate-level program of study that includes, at a minimum, a practicum-type course covering administration and interpretation of standardized test of academic achievement. In addition, many qualified examiners possess state, provincial, or professional certification, registration, or licensure in the field or profession that includes as a part of its formal training and code of ethics the responsibility for rendering an educational assessment and interpretation services.

(McGrew et al. 2014: 10)

12 Ethics and Foundational Practices

Competent interpretation of the WJ-IV-ACH requires "a higher degree of knowledge and experience than is required for administering and scoring the tests" (ibid.). "Graduate-level training in educational assessment and a background in diagnostic decision-making are recommended for individuals who will interpret" (ibid.). "Only trained and knowledgeable professionals who are sensitive to the conditions that may compromise, or invalidate test results should make interpretations and decisions" (ibid.).

Similarly, WIAT-III users "have a significant responsibility to ensure the accuracy and thoroughness of the test administration in order to protect social and legal rights for the individual whose achievement is assessed" (WIAT-III 2009: 6) and "Examiners who do not have formal training and assessment can administer the subtest scores and responses under the supervision of an experience professional. Only individuals who have received professional training and educational psychological assessment should interpret the results of the WIAT-III" (WIAT-III 2009: 6).

The Association of Educational Therapy is very diligent in monitoring that members are operating within its Code of Ethics. The Scope of Practice/Ethics Committee is prominently displayed on the website's Board Organizational Chart; the Ethics Complaint Procedure is readily available on the website as it the Ethics Complaint Form for reporting any possible violation. Confirmed ethics violations are dealt with swiftly and by communicating and cooperating with any state or other professional organization. Training programs are required to instruct regarding the ethical standards of AET. Supervision requires a review of the Code of Ethics and Professional Members are required to document participation in an ethics workshop every six years. Those seeking to fulfill the requirements to become a Board Certified Member, sit for a Best Practices Exam that focuses on ethical issues. "Written responses to exam questions will require the candidate to demonstrate good judgment regarding complex ethical issues, as well as to provide substantial support of examples from the candidate's own background of experiences" (Association of Educational Therapists 2017).

Publishers have their own established criteria for who may purchase instruments. These may also guide the ET. If you cannot sufficiently document your training, you will not be allowed to purchase some tests and you should *not* be giving them. Do not borrow instruments from others if you do not have adequate formal training in assessment. "This training should result in a basic understanding of test statistics, general procedures governing test administration, scoring, and interpretation" (Wiederholt & Bryant 2012: 5) and "previous experience administering similar measures" (ibid.).

Publishers separate assessment instruments into three categories. They are rated as Level A, B, and C tests. Contrary to school grading classifications, the order is reversed. Nearly anyone can administer an A Level test. ETs with a Master's degree and graduate-level training in assessment may purchase and use B level tests and C level tests are generally cognitive instruments and additional advanced training and documentation is required to purchase, administer and interpret these (see Table 2.1).

Ethics and Foundational Practices 13

Table 2.1 Examiner's Qualifications

Level A	Level B	Level C
• No special qualifications needed • May be administered to groups	• Master's degree in psychology, education, or a closely related field and formal training in ethical administration, scoring, and interpretation • Certification by, or full active membership in, a professional organization that requires training and experience in assessment	• Doctorate in psychology, education, or a closely related field and formal training in ethical administration, scoring, and interpretation *or* • Licensure or certification to practice in your state in a field related to the purchase

In summary, "AET members participate in an organization that maintains high professional standards in the interdisciplinary fields of educational therapy" (AET Code of Ethics) and have established clear boundaries for it is members in conducting assessment.

Other Ethical Concerns

The author is frequently asked, "I get a great ideal of information from using an older edition of an assessment instrument because I know it so well. May I continue to use it?" No. You should purchase the latest edition within six months (some publishers allow one year) if you intend to continue using that instrument. Why? The norms are out of date. Individual items and topics in reading passages become dated. Assessment authors continuously evaluate what constructs should be measured. And subsequent editions undergo significant reconstruction in response to critiques about the assessment's reliability and validity from outside evaluators such as those printed in the Buros *Mental Measurement Yearbook* (see below). You are disregarding all the possible new information that you could be obtaining by using an out-of-date edition. Perhaps if one is treating the older edition as an informal measure, it might be possible to use it. *Do not* report the scores to any others if using an older edition (including consumable materials) as it is not professional.

Additionally, photocopying test materials is illegal and a breach of professional ethics. Do not photocopy tests or the consumable materials (Marshall & Matthaei 2013). Photocopying student forms may reduce the visual clarity of the copy from which the student works. That may impact the results and invalidate the norms.

14 Ethics and Foundational Practices

When purchasing a standardized instrument, note that assessors must "ensure the security of test material. Do not display test materials. Test materials may not be resold or displayed in locations where unqualified individuals can purchase or view partial or completed portions" (WIAT-III 2009: 6).

Lastly, giving individually administered standardized instruments requires *informed consent*. This means that an adult client or a child's parent or guardian must be informed that you wish to administer a test or group of measures, have received a brief description of each test, and give permission *in writing* before one can assess.

Foundational Practices in Administering Standardized Assessments

There are many keystones in administering standardized assessment instruments. Each aspect is critical to the process and requires training and practice (this list is based on Marshall & Matthaei 2013).

Foundational Skills

1 Formulate which questions an assessment will attempt to answer.
2 Determine the assessment battery.
3 Review test instructions before each session. Test must be administered correctly and uniformly to obtain valid results. Review the instructions for prompting, repeating directions, etc.
4 Work to establish rapport with the student.
5 Be friendly and pleasant. Tell the student what to expect. Be consistent, observant, and impartial. Assess, *do not* teach, during the assessment. If a student appears to be ill or there are other extenuating circumstances, discontinue testing until a time when the test results can be considered a fair and representative measure.
6 Administer each test correctly. If the test contains several tests or subtests, it is best to give each part in the order indicated. If allowed to administer selected parts, best practice is to administer them in the order given in the complete assessment.
7 Record all student responses in a consistent manner to avoid unintentionally cueing for correct responses. Praise for *effort* not for correctness of responses.
8 Note and record behaviors during assessment including:

- Level of student's concentration.
- Level of engagement to the task.
- Level of persistence, even when the task was difficult.
- Response style (such as impulsive, thoughtful, hesitant, request for information to be repeated, etc.) Remember that the student's response style may vary when different tasks are presented and this is important to note.

Ethics and Foundational Practices 15

9 Record the spontaneous comments of the student made during the assessment (see Chapter 4).
10 Score each assessment correctly. Understand test construction, validity, reliability, test–retest relationship, standard error of measurement, testing bias and cross-cultural fairness (see Chapter 3).
11 Understand the meaning of different types of scores, especially standard scores and percentile rank (see Chapter 3).
12 Avoid using age- and grade-level equivalents (see Chapter 3).
13 Perform item analyses, looking for patterns of strengths and weaknesses
14 Integrate information from multiple sources—the results from a variety of instruments, parents, allied professionals' reports, and relevant background information including health history and reports from schools and/or other professionals.
15 Write in a professional voice (see Chapter 5).
16 Use the Findings to create and prioritize useful and appropriate recommendations, interventions, materials and strategies (see Chapter 4).
17 Demonstrate knowledge of professional and ethical standards of assessment.
18 Refer to allied professionals, as indicated by the assessment results.
19 Prepare to conduct a well-organized, appropriately paced, empathetic Report of Findings meeting (see Chapter 6).

Reflective Questions for ET Students and Professionals

- What are the standards for ETs when conducting assessment?
- When is the next time you should participate in an AET Ethics workshop?
- What do ET training programs need to provide to ensure adequate preparation in assessment?
- Is it permissible to share assessment instruments? If yes, under what circumstances?
- Make a list of your assessment practices. Compare them to the foundational practices listed above. Are there any aspects you need to review, adjust, or redress?

Which Standardized Assessments Measure Reading, Written Expression, Mathematics and Processing Skills?

Whether you are deciding which standardized assessment(s) to use with a student or are reading a report conducted by someone else, you may need guidance about the different achievement tests and what each measures. Many students are surprised to learn that ETs may give some tests which measure the processing skills that undergird learning. Part 3 is designed to assist you in all of these endeavors. Listed are assessment instruments that (1) all ETs who qualify to purchase B Level tests may use (or the equivalent), and (2) are tests that been reviewed by the Buros *Mental Measurement Yearbook* (MMY). Test descriptions are from the publisher's website. All assessments instruments in this book were the current edition, when the book was published.

16 *Ethics and Foundational Practices*

About the Mental Measurements Yearbook

The MMY, produced by the Buros Institute at the University of Nebraska, provides users with a comprehensive guide to over 2,700 contemporary testing instruments. Designed for an audience ranging from novice test consumers to experienced professionals, the MMY series contains information essential for a complete evaluation of test products within such diverse areas as psychology, education, business, and leadership. First published by Oscar K. Buros, the MMY series allows users to make knowledgeable judgments and informed selection decisions about the increasingly complex world of testing (see www.ebsco.com/products/research-databases/mental-measurements-yearbook).

As you read the excerpts of each MMY review (available online from most university libraries), understand that many pages are devoted to the technical aspects and "worthiness." Test worthiness evaluates whether the assessment instrument meets standards in several key areas: validity, reliability, cross-cultural fairness, and practicality for the assessor. According to Neukrug & Fawcett (2009: 62), the MMY is considered a "tremendous resource in finding and selecting tests." The following definitions are based on Neukrug & Fawcett (2009: 43).

- **Validity**—whether the test measures what it purports to measure. Content validity and construct validity are both considered in determining validity.
- **Reliability**—whether the score of an individual is "an accurate measure of her/his true score." Test–retest reliability and whether parallel forms are equivalent are important.
- **Cross-cultural fairness**—whether test results are a "true reflection of that individual and not a function of cultural bias inherent in the test."
- **Practicality**—factors concerning ease of administration, time to administer the instrument, test format, cost, and scoring are key considerations.

A complete description of each of these is available in the full review from Buros.

Which Standardized Assessments Measure Reading?

Gray Oral Reading Test, 5th Edition (GORT-5)

www.proedinc.com

Description: The GORT-5 (Wiederholt & Bryant 2012) has two equivalent forms: Form A and Form B. Each form contains 16 developmentally sequenced reading passages with five comprehension questions each. It may be used to:

1 Identify students who may need more intensive or explicit instruction in reading in order to make adequate progress in reading facility and/or comprehension.

2 Diagnose specific reading disabilities in children through young adults.
3 Compare intra-individual reading skills (e.g., reading rate vs. comprehension) and to help tailor interventions to the student's specific
   needs.
4 Evaluate students' progress in reading using pre-and post-intervention
   testing.

ESSENTIAL DETAILS

Administration time: 20–30 minutes
Scores: Rate, Accuracy, Fluency (Rate and Accuracy combined), Comprehension,
and an Oral Reading Index (a composite of Fluency and Comprehension).
Publication date: 2012
Ages: 6:0–23:11

MMY REVIEW

Volume 20
  Reviewer: Gabriel Della-Piana

> The GORT-5 is a well standardized, normed, and individually adminis-
> tered test of oral reading Rate, Accuracy, Fluency, Comprehension ... It
> has high reliability for the intended uses in placement decisions, instruc-
> tional decisions, and research on and evaluation of interventions. Validity
> evidence related to content, concurrent, and construct approaches to vali-
> dation is generally very good.
>
> (Della-Piana 2017)

Kaufman Test of Educational Achievement, 3rd Edition (KTEA-3)

Pearsonassessment.com

Description: Evaluates academic skills in reading, math, written language, and
oral language. Can be used to identify learning disabilities, achievement gaps
and measure progress. Items align with IDEA and National Council of Teachers of Mathematics (NCTM).

ESSENTIAL DETAILS

Administration time: 15–85 minutes
Scores: Age- and grade-based standard scores, age and grade equivalents, per-
centile ranks, normal curve equivalents, stanines, and Growth Scale Value
Publication date: 2018
Ages: 4:00–25:11

18 *Ethics and Foundational Practices*

MMY REVIEW

Volume 20
   Reviewers: Merilee McCurdy and Leslie Hart

The Kaufman Test of Educational Achievement, Third Edition (KTEA-3), is a thoroughly planned, user-friendly instrument that can be very helpful for school based practitioners or those assisting young adults in planning for their futures. The test presents good statistics in both reliability and validity studies. The test battery covers all of the areas necessary to have a good understanding of an examinee's academic strengths and weaknesses. It is also helpful to use the error analysis to determine eligibility for services and goals.

(McCurdy & Hart 2017)

Nelson-Denny Reading Test (NDRT), Forms I & J

www.wpspublish.com

Description: Measures silent reading vocabulary, comprehension, and rate

ESSENTIAL DETAILS

Administration time: 35–56 minutes
Scores: Age- and grade-equivalent scores, percentile ranks, and index scores
Publication date: 2018
Ages: High School to 2-year and 4-year colleges

At this time, the MMY review is only available for the outdated (1993) edition, so it is not summarized here.

Process Assessment of the Learner, 2nd Edition: Diagnostics for Reading and Writing (PAL-II)

Pearsonassessment.com

Description: A multi-tier, research-based assessment, intervention, and progress monitoring system for reading and writing. It can be used to diagnose dysgraphia, dyslexia, oral and written language disability. PAL-II Reading and Writing links to targeted evidenced-based interventions and lessons.

ESSENTIAL DETAILS

Administration time: "time varies based on the subtests selected by the examiner"

Scores: Scaled scores and cumulative percentages
Publication date: 2007
Grades: K–6th

MMY REVIEW

Volume 18
Reviewer: S. Kathleen Krach

> The wide variety of assessments of processing in reading and writing in the PAL-II RW may provide a more nuanced look at children's performance in these areas than other tests. However, it is unwieldy to administer, score, and interpret. The user's guide must be consulted, but it is not accessible to all users. A serious weakness of the test is the exclusion of students with or perceived to be at risk for reading or writing failure from the norming group and all tests of reliability and validity. This is puzzling in an assessment that the manual repeatedly claims is designed to identify such students and diagnose their problems.
>
> (Krach 2010)

Test of Word Reading Efficiency, 2nd Edition (TOWRE-2)

Pearsonassessment.com

Description: Test of Word Reading Efficiency Second Edition is a measure of an individual's ability to pronounce printed words and phonemically regular nonwords accurately and fluently. Assesses the number of real printed words that can be accurately identified within 45 seconds. It measures the number of pronounceable printed non-words that can be accurately decoded within 45 seconds.

ESSENTIAL DETAILS

Administration time: 5 minutes
Scores: standard scores, percentile ranks, and age and grade equivalents
Publication date: 2012
Ages: 6:0–24:11

MMY REVIEW

Volume 20
Reviewer: Gina L. Harrison

> TOWRE-2 is a well-designed update to the original TOWRE assessing two areas predictive of reading development and proficiency ... It

20   *Ethics and Foundational Practices*

represents a useful tool within the examiner's assessment repertoire as part of a multifaceted comprehensive assessment of reading. The addition of two new forms greatly enhances its progress-monitoring utility.

(Harrison 2017)

The Wechsler Individual Achievement Test, 3rd Edition (WIAT-III)

Pearsonassessments.com

Description: The WIAT-III is an achievement test for use in a variety of clinical, educational and research settings, including schools, clinics, private practices and residential treatment facilities.[It may be used to] Identify student academic abilities, make educational placement decisions, diagnose specific learning disability, design instructional objectives, and plan interventions. It measures all eight areas of achievement specified by IDEA legislation. Can be used to evaluate patterns of strengths and weaknesses to identify learning disabilities. Correlated with the following ability measures: WISC-V and WAIS-IV.

ESSENTIAL DETAILS

Administration time: 35 minutes (pre K)–104 minutes
Scores: norm referenced and criterion referenced information.
Publication date: 2009 (currently fielding testing WIAT IV)
Ages: 4:00–50:11
Subtests which measure reading:

Grade 1 Reading Comprehension, Word Reading, Pseudoword Decoding
Grade 2–12 Reading Comprehension, Word Reading, Pseudoword Decoding, Oral Reading Fluency

MMY REVIEW

Volume 18
Reviewer: M. David Miller

The WIAT-III appears to be a well-developed assessment. There is a fair amount of theoretical justification for inclusion of the various subtests. There is a great deal of empirical support for the reliability of the assessment, as well as a strong start to the process of validation with the intended population. The materials that accompany the assessment are extensive and very useful. Further, much of the research from the previous edition will be broadly applicable to this edition as well. Reviews of those previous editions are available and should be consulted.

(Miller 2010)

The Wide Range Achievement Test, 5th Edition (WRAT5)

Pearsonassessments.com

Description: It provides an accurate and easy-to-administer way to assess and monitor reading, spelling, and math skills, and helps identify possible learning disabilities. Screen individuals or small groups (with some subtests) to help identify those requiring a more comprehensive academic achievement evaluation.

ESSENTIAL DETAILS

Administration time: Approximately 15 to 25 minutes for ages 5 to 7, and 30 to 40 minutes for ages 8 and up
Scores: Math Computation: measures an individual's ability to count, identify numbers, solve simple oral math problems, and calculate written math problems with a time limit. A Reading Composite score is created by combining the Word Reading and Sentence Comprehension standard scores.
Publication date: 2017
Ages: 5–85+

MMY REVIEW

Volume 18
  Reviewer: George Engelhard

> As far back as the first edition in 1946, critics have suggested, "that the test is misnamed, that as a measure of school achievement it has doubtful value" (Sims, 1949, p. 47). We believe it might be better to consider the WRAT a measure of ability rather than academic achievement, and as such, the range of non-school ages targeted for the test can be better understood. However, should the test be better understood as a measure of ability, the addition of grade-based norms for a test that has traditionally been marketed with age-based norms becomes questionable. Likewise, the interpretation of grade equivalents becomes untenable.
>
> (Engelhard 2010)

Woodcock–Johnson IV Tests of Achievement (WJ-IV-ACH)

www.hmhco.com/~/media/sites/home/hmh-assessments/clinical/Wood cock–Johnson/pdf/wjiv/wj_iv_author_newsletter_winter_2014.pdf?la=en

Description: The WJ-IV-ACH includes 20 tests for measuring four broad academic domains: reading, written language, mathematics, and academic knowledge. A completely new configuration, with new tests and clusters, supports a broad range of diagnostic assessment needs for a wide variety of professionals…

22 *Ethics and Foundational Practices*

A new comparison of achievement scores to academic knowledge can provide additional information to help determine if a more comprehensive evaluation should be considered. Eleven of the most frequently used achievement tests are included in the Standard Battery, which has three parallel forms. There is a single form of the Extended Battery containing nine additional diagnostic measures that can be used with any form of the Standard Battery.

Tests of reading: Letter–Word Identification, Word Attack, Passage Comprehension, Reading Recall, Reading Vocabulary, Oral Reading, Sentence Reading Fluency.

ESSENTIAL DETAILS

Administration time: 5–10 minutes per subtest (test)
Scores: The Score Report provides age equivalent (AE) scores (including difficulty levels or ranges), relative proficiency index (RPI), and standard score or percentile rank for a single examinee.
Publication date: 2014
Ages: 2–90+

MMY REVIEW

Volume 20
   Reviewer: Gary L. Canivez

> The Woodcock–Johnson IV (WJ-IV) is a collection of three distinct individually administered test batteries constructed to be consistent with Cattell–Horn–Carroll (CHC) theory of cognitive abilities ... The three batteries were co–normed and include the Woodcock–Johnson IV Tests of Cognitive Abilities (WJ-IV-COG), the Woodcock–Johnson IV Tests of Achievement (WJ-IV-ACH), and the Woodcock–Johnson IV Tests of Oral Language (WJ-IV-OL). Oral language may be assessed in English and Spanish. The three batteries may be used individually or in any combination. The WJ IV is a major revision of its predecessor, the Woodcock–Johnson III ... The WJ IV appears a good measure of general intelligence and provides useful measures of academic achievement, which may well be how the WJ IV will be primarily used.
>
> (Canivez 2017)

Which Standardized Tests Measure Written Language?

Test of Early Written Language, 3rd Edition (TEWL-3)

Pearsonassessment.com

Description: Administered independently to measure a child's understanding of language and ability to use the writing tools of language, construct a story, or overall writing ability. Aligns with TOWL-4 and extends the assessment range to younger children.

ESSENTIAL DETAILS

Administration time: 30–50 minutes
Scores: standard score indexes (M = 100, SD = 15) for age and grade percentiles, and age and grade equivalents.
Publication date: 2012
Ages: 4:00–10:11

MMY REVIEW

Volume 20
  Reviewer: Sharon H. de Fur

> TEWL-3 is a fairly short measure of writing or emerging writing that may be used to identify children lagging in writing skills. Its technical foundation, though not completely documented, is nevertheless very good. Users can be confident that scores will be sufficiently reliable for individual decisions, and within the limitations of the stated purposes, the scores should be useful. Additional validity information would be helpful, as would advice on identifying plausible interventions when deficiencies are noted. The test authors have addressed many of the concerns raised by reviews of TEWL-2. As a result, the TEWL-3 is superior to its predecessors and could prove helpful when a standardized tool for writing proficiency is needed for younger children.
>
> (De Fur 2017)

Test of Integrated Language and Literacy Skills (TILLS)

Description: "TILLS is a comprehensive, norm-referenced test that has been standardized to identify oral and written language & literacy disorders."

ESSENTIAL DETAILS

Administration time: 90 minutes
Scores: Standard Scores and Percentile Ranks
Publication date: 2016
Ages: 6–18

MMY REVIEW

Volume 20
  Reviewer: M. J. Moyle

24   *Ethics and Foundational Practices*

The Test of Integrated Language and Literacy Skills (TILLS) is a comprehensive, individually administered assessment of oral and written language skills for students ages 6 to 18 years. The TILLS is a psychometrically sound assessment based on current theoretical models of language and literacy. It is thoughtfully designed and appears to serve its three primary purposes: identify language and literacy disorders, document patterns of relative strengths and weaknesses, and track changes in language and literacy skills over time. The TILLS is not appropriate for use with students who are not native English speakers and those whose cultural backgrounds and experiences differ substantially from the normative sample.

(Moyle 2016)

Test of Written Language, 4th Edition (TOWL-4)

Description: "A norm-referenced comprehensive diagnostic test of written expression" and "TOWL-4 offers seven subtests to help you assess the conventional, linguistic, and conceptual aspects of students' writing."

ESSENTIAL DETAILS

Administration time: 60–90 minutes
Scores: Composite scores for Overall Writing, Contrived Writing, and Spontaneous Writing
Publication date: 2009
Ages: 9:0–17:11

MMY REVIEW

Volume 20
  Reviewer: Felicia Castro-Villareal

The TOWL-4 is a comprehensive and effective measure of written language designed to assess both contrived and spontaneous writing formats. It has an adequate standardization sample of children and adolescents ages 9 years, 0 months to 17 years, 11 months (Grades 4–11). The test authors should be commended for successfully minimizing the subjectivity in scoring procedures ... and providing extensive reliability and validity data to support its utility. This measure provides clinicians and other professionals with a reliable and valid measure of written expression.

(Castro-Villareal 2017)

The Wechsler Individual Achievement Test, 3rd Edition (WIAT-III)

Pearsonassessments.com

Kindergarten—Alphabet Writing Fluency, Spelling

Grade 1 & 2—Alphabet Writing Fluency, Sentence Composition, Spelling
Grade 3—Alphabet Writing Fluency, Sentence Composition, Essay Composition, Spelling
Grade 4–12—Sentence Composition, Essay Composition, Spelling
  See Reading Tests for description, essential details, and MMY review.

Woodcock–Johnson IV Tests of Achievement (WJ-IV-ACH)

www.riverside-assessments.com

Tests: Writing Samples, Sentence Writing Fluency, Spelling, Spelling of Sounds, Editing.
  See Reading Tests for description, essential details, and MMY review.

The Wide Range Achievement Test, 5th Edition (WRAT5)

Subtest: Spelling (only Written Language measure).

See Reading Tests for description, essential details, and MMY review.

Which Standardized Tests Measure Mathematics?

Key Math-3 Diagnostic Assessment

Pearsonassessment.com

Description: KeyMath-3 Diagnostic Assessment is an individually administered measure of essential mathematical concepts and skills. It consists of three linked components: The updated KeyMath-3 Diagnostic Assessment, ASSIST Scoring and Reporting Software, and the KeyMath-3 Essential Resources instructional program.

ESSENTIAL DETAILS

Administration time: 30–90 minutes
Scores: Areas and Total Test: Grade-and age-based standard scores ($M = 100$, $SD = 15$), grade and age equivalents, percentile ranks and Growth Scale Values. Subtests: Grade- and age-based scale scores ($M = 10$, $SD = 3$), and grade and age equivalents.
Publication date: 2007
Ages: 4:6–21:11; Grades K–12

MMY REVIEW

Volume 18
  Reviewer: Graham Laughlin

26 Ethics and Foundational Practices

The KeyMath-3 Diagnostic Assessment is an individually administered test that is well developed and provides scores that can inform the design of individual student intervention programs and monitor performance over time. The manual is well written and provides clear guidelines for administering, scoring, and interpreting the scores. The technical information provided in the manual is comprehensive, clearly presented, and supports the use of the instrument for its purpose.

(Laughlin 2010)

Process Assessment of the Learner II PAL-II M

Pearsonassessment.com

Description: The Process Assessment of the Learner Second Edition: Diagnostics for Math measures the development of cognitive processes critical to learning math skills and actual math performance. PAL-II Math is appropriate as either Tier 1, Tier 2 or Tier 3 evaluation tool.

ESSENTIAL DETAILS

Administration time: "Varies depending on subtests selected by the examiner"
Scores: Normed using Scaled Scores and base rates
Publication date: 2007
Grades: K–6

MMY REVIEW

Volume 18
Reviewer: Laura Hamilton

The great strength of the PAL-II lies not in national standardization but in the rich diagnostic information provided by its many subtests of basic math-related processes. In the end, educators care less about how a student compares with national norms than about what specifically hinders a student's progress in learning and how to target interventions to overcome students' individual difficulties. The significant contribution of the PAL-II to the psychometric and educational communities is its many subtests that disentangle the highly integrated basic processes of mathematics in order to determine specific causes of students' learning difficulties, which can be particularly useful in the middle grades, when students may not have achieved fluency in basic skills, but mathematics instruction has progressed beyond basic to higher level skills. The PAL-II has been designed from the beginning to assist educators in identifying the right interventions for struggling students, and has great potential for helping all students succeed.

(Hamilton 2010)

Test of Early Math Ability (TEMA 3)

www.parinc.com

Description: The TEMA-3 can be used to measure progress, evaluate programs, screen for readiness, discover the basis for poor mathematics performance, identify gifted students, and guide instruction and remediation. It measures informal and formal (school-taught) concepts and skills in the areas of numbering skills, number-comparison facility, numeral literacy, mastery of number facts, calculation skills, and understanding of concepts. A book of remedial techniques (*Assessment Probes and Instructional Activities*) includes numerous teaching tasks for skills covered by each TEMA-3 item.

ESSENTIAL DETAILS

Administration time: 40 minutes
Scores: Standard scores, percentile ranks, and age and grade equivalents
Publication date: 2003
Ages: 3–8:11 years

MMY REVIEW

Volume 16
  Reviewer: Kevin D. Crehan

> With each new successive edition of the TEMA, the test is improved. The theory and research base supporting the test is strong. The test is user friendly. All materials are included in the packet with clear directions for use. Administration and scoring instructions are clearly spelled out ... The technical characteristics continue to improve as the authors expand the norming samples and include additional reliability and validity studies. Nonetheless there is still room for improvement. Validity evidence linked to the recommended test uses would strengthen the test and bring the validity studies more in line with the current standards ... Overall, this is a strong tool in the repertoire of tests of the mathematical knowledge of young children.

(Crehan 2005)

Test of Mathematical Abilities, 3rd Edition (TOMA-3)

Description: The *Test of Mathematical Abilities* 3rd edition (TOMA-3) is an easily administered, norm-referenced, assessment tool used to identify,

28 Ethics and Foundational Practices

describe, and quantify mathematical deficits in school age children. Specifically, it can be used to identify students who are significantly behind their peers in mathematical knowledge and to determine the magnitude (below average, poor, or very poor) of any mathematical problems.

ESSENTIAL DETAILS

Administration time: 60–90 minutes
Scores: mathematical ability index, age and grade equivalents, subtest scaled scores, percentile ranks and SEMs.
Publication Date: 2018
Ages: 8:0–18:11 years

MMY REVIEW

Volume 20
   Reviewer: Thomas J. Gross

> The TOMA-3 provides a quality assessment of the mathematical skills of school-aged children. The test authors indicated the primary use of this test is to identify students with mathematical difficulties and determine the extent of the difficulty. It is unclear how useful this measure is to educators and how the TOMA-3 is used in school settings. Broad assessment measures (e.g., Woodcock–Johnson Tests of Achievement; Wechsler Individual Achievement Test) or curriculum-based measures commonly are used in the identification of learning disabilities. The TOMA-3 could be used in follow up assessments to determine specific areas of mathematical deficits.
>
> (Gross 2017)

The Wechsler Individual Achievement Test, 3rd Edition (WIAT-III)

Pearsonassessments.com

Subtests: Math Fluency—Addition, Math Fluency—Subtraction, Numerical Operations, Math Problem Solving.

See Reading Tests for description, essential details, and MMY review.

Woodcock–Johnson IV Tests of Achievement (WJ-IV-ACH)

Tests: Math Fact Fluency, Math Calculation Skills, (Problem Solving = Applied Problems, Number Matrices).

See Reading Tests for description, essential details, and MMY review.

Ethics and Foundational Practices 29

Standardized Tests that Measure Processing Skills

Beery-Buktenica Test of Visual Motor Integration, 6th Edition (VMI-6)

www.pearsonassessments.com

Description: Internationally respected and backed by decades of research and clinical use, the Beery-Buktenica Developmental Test of Visual-Motor Integration, Sixth Edition (BEERY VMI) helps assess the extent to which individuals can integrate their visual and motor abilities. Use with individuals of diverse environmental, educational, and linguistic backgrounds as a culture-free, non-verbal assessment.

ESSENTIAL DETAILS

Administration time: 10–15 minutes
Scores: Standardized on a national sample with proven reliability and validity
Beery VMI, Visual Perception (optional), Motor Coordination (optional).
Publication date: 2013
Ages: 2–99

MMY REVIEW

Volume 19
    Reviewer: Michael G. Poteat

> The Beery VMI remains a useful instrument some 40-plus years after it was first published ... It is easy to administer and has good reliability and adequate validity. For its primary intended purpose as a screening instrument to identify children with visual-motor integration deficits, the Beery VMI may be the best choice of instruments currently available. In addition to providing normative information about the visual-motor integration of children, it also provides an opportunity for the examiner to observe certain important behaviors. Some examples include the pencil grasp employed, the reaction to more difficult forms, perseverance and perseveration, and attention to detail.
>
> (Poteat 2007)

Comprehensive Test of Phonological Processing Skills, 2nd Edition (CTOPP-2)

www.pearsonassessments.com

Description: CTOPP-2 includes twelve subtests plus supplemental tests to assess specific phonological strengths and weaknesses are included. Applicable

30 *Ethics and Foundational Practices*

across two age levels: 4–6 and 7–24. The Comprehensive Test of Phonological Processing Second Edition (CTOPP-2) helps evaluate phonological processing abilities as a prerequisite to reading fluency.

ESSENTIAL DETAILS

Administration time: 40 minutes
Scores: Subtest scaled scores, percentile ranks, age and grade equivalents, composite indexes, and developmental scores
Publication date: 2013
Ages: 4–24

MMY REVIEW

Volume 20
   Reviewer: Steven H. Blaustein

> The CTOPP-2 is a revision of the CTOPP that was published to meet the need for an assessment of reading-related phonological processing skills. It is to be used to identify individuals functioning below peers in phonological abilities, to determine areas of strength and weakness among phonological processes, to monitor progress for those receiving intervention, and as a measure to be used in research ... The test developers clearly note that the CTOPP-2 should not stand alone to arrive at a diagnosis and should be used in conjunction with multiple assessment measures to gain an understanding of possible deficits in phonological processing in an individual. With an understanding of the variables involved in phonological processing and the model and construction of the test, the CTOPP-2 can be of value in assessing phonological processing as part of a larger assessment battery incorporating a variety of standardized assessment measures and authentic assessment.
>
> (Blaustein 2017)

Rapid Automatized Naming and Rapid Alternating Stimulus Tests (RAN/ RAS)

www.proedinc.com

Description: The RAN and RAS Tests are individually administered measures designed to estimate an individual's ability to recognize a visual symbol such as a letter or color and name it accurately and rapidly. The tests consist of rapid automatized naming tests (Letters, Numbers, Colors, Objects) and two rapid alternating stimulus tests. Scores are based on the amount of time required to name all of the stimulus items on each test.

Essential Details

Administration time: 5–10 minutes
Scores: percentiles, standard scores, and age and grade equivalents
Publication Date: 2005
Ages: 5:0–18:11

MMY Review

Volume 17
  Reviewer: Russell N. Carney

> The Rapid Automatized Naming and Rapid Alternating Stimulus Tests (RAN/RAS Tests) are based on 30 years of research and clinical evidence. They constitute quick, easily administered, reliable measures of naming speed. And of more importance, the tests appear to be valid for their stated purposes: identifying children at risk for reading/learning problems, ongoing assessment, and the measurement of children's word-retrieval systems.
>
> (Carney 2007)

Test of Auditory Processing Skills, 4th Edition (TAPS-4)

www.proedinc.com

Description: The TAPS-4 provides information about language processing and comprehension skills across three intersecting areas: phonological processing, auditory memory and listening comprehension.

Essential Details

Administration time: 60–90 minutes
Scores: scaled scores for subtests, standard scores for indices
Publication Date: 2018
Ages: 5–21

MMY Review

Volume 18
  Reviewers: Timothy R. Konold and Rebecca Blanchard
  This is the review of the TAPS-3 since there is not a current one for the TAPS-4.

> The instrument appears easy to administer and score, and perhaps of most importance, there is some evidence to suggest that it does a good job

32 *Ethics and Foundational Practices*

discriminating between children with and without auditory processing problems ... Demonstrating the extent to which scores are free from error (reliability) and that the scores are appropriate for their intended use (validity) is an ongoing process. The examiner's manual addresses several important psychometric issues relating to the interpretation of scores and appropriateness of use with this population of children. Although some of the reported results are promising, there is room for improvement. Several of the internal consistency estimates for some subtests and age groups were below contemporary standards.

(Konold & Blanchard 2010)

A test is a tool used to sample an individual's performance at a given time in a particular situation. Even the best test does not reveal *why* an individual performed as s/he did.

(Hammill & Larsen 2009: 53; emphasis added)

Test Format and the Learner's Profile

Although it is very useful to know what each test assesses in each academic area, test construction or the test's format can influence test results. Students can perform very differently on tests whose names sound very similar and whose purpose seems nearly identical. The way a student interacts with and responds to assessment prompts are key to understanding a student's scores.

Let us compare two well-regarded tests with similar sounding names—the WJ-IV-ACH's "Passage Comprehension" test and the WIAT-III's "Reading Comprehension" subtest.

On WJ-IV-ACH's "Passage Comprehension," the student is prompted to read silently "passages" which increase in complexity of semantics, sentence construction, and vocabulary. Only one "passage" is three sentences long. (All items increase in their sentence complexity but most are only two sentences long.) The student is required to fill in the missing word in the passage. This is known as the "cloze procedure." Contrast that with the format of WIAT-III's "Reading Comprehension" subtest where the student reads aloud a variety of types of texts (stories, science and history) and other genres, including advertisements. Students need to interpret tables and graphs, as well. The reading items are all closely aligned to those seen and practiced in the student's grade-level school setting.

Might the reading orally or reading "silently" influence the resulting scores? Could the length of the passage affect the student's score? On the WIAT-III's "Reading Comprehension" subtest, the student is allowed to look back at the text to answer the comprehension questions. That is a reading strategy commonly taught in schools. In contrast, there are *no* comprehension questions asked on the WJ-IV-ACH's "Passage Comprehension" test. Instead, the student must utilize background knowledge, vocabulary, and understanding of English syntax and

Ethics and Foundational Practices 33

grammar to "fill in" the missing word. Might that impact a student's score? Could a lack of familiarity with this type of exercise impact the score?

If one adds in the format and prompts of the Gray Oral Reading Test, GORT 5, a different picture emerges. The GORT-5 is also designed measure a student's reading comprehension, along with reading rate and reading accuracy. The student reads passages of increasing length and complexity. The student is timed while reading *aloud*. Comprehension questions are varied in type—recall, understanding of specific vocabulary, and the ability to draws inferences from what has just been read. The student *may not refer* back to the passage to aid in recall. Might being timed affect one's scores? Could not being able to "look back" impact the reading comprehension score? Do you see that the construction and format of these three tests might have an effect on the student's reading comprehension score? It is startling to consider that the very same student might score wildly differently on these commonly used measures of reading comprehension. Are the student's strengths and weaknesses in reading comprehension *accurately* being measured? Reflect on how the learning profile of a student might be *impacted* or *benefit* from each test's format. Create this understanding for each test or subtest you administer. A novice assessor may be content with administering and scoring a test or subtest correctly. Of course, this is imperative. However, the experienced assessor recognizes and considers the student's learning profile and the potential effect of the assessment task itself.

Reflective Task

Think about how these factors might affect a student's performance on a reading comprehension test:

- reading orally or "silently"
- whether timed or untimed
- can the reader refer back to the text?
- the size of font in the text
- the amount of words on a page
- the length of the passage
- whether the passage is narrative (fiction) or expository (non-fiction)
- the type of questions being asked (recall, multiple choice, vocabulary, making inferences)
- whether the instrument uses a cloze format

Mini Case Studies

The following case studies are designed to encourage thinking about the interface between a test's format and the learner's profile.

34 Ethics and Foundational Practices

"Carlita" is in the 4th grade and attends a local independent school. By report, she is good natured, has many friends and is a sought-after soccer player. Her first language was Spanish. When reading new material, she mispronounces many words which embarrasses her, so she prefers not to be called on to read aloud in class. Her teacher is concerned about her reading comprehension now that more expository texts are being introduced into the curriculum. The school's educational therapist decides to give her the GORT-5 to evaluate her reading skills. Her "Rate" is average (33rd percentile rank). Carlita's "Accuracy" is below average for her age (17th percentile rank). Her "Fluency" score is average (45th percentile rank) and her "Comprehension" is below average (10th percentile rank), according to the Scaled Scores and descriptors associated with the GORT-5. The resulting "Oral Reading Index" ("Fluency" and "Comprehension" combined) is below average.

The examiner noted that Carlita's reading was fluent and she could answer nearly all of the comprehension questions in the earlier passages. Her reading became halting and her reading volume dropped to "almost whisper like" when the passages were approaching or were at her grade level. Then, she struggled to answer many of the comprehension questions.

Questions for Students and Professionals

1 Was this the best choice of reading test to administer to Carlita? Why or why not?
2 Do you think her scores on the GORT-5 are an accurate reflection of her reading skills?
3 If you were to pair another reading test with the GORT-5, what might you use? Why would you chose it?

"Nicky" is a sixth-grader and is reported to have a good fund of general knowledge and is keenly interested in animals and in science because he "wants to understand how things work." The ET tells you that he checked out all of the Eyewitness books (which contain detailed illustrated pictures) "over and over again" in elementary school. He shares that he wants to be a veterinarian. His father has referred him to you, because Nicky is having difficulty keeping up with all the different types of readings assigned as homework. And he tells you that Nicky was diagnosed with ADHD last year. You decide to use the "Passage Comprehension" test of the WJ IV Achievement Test to evaluate his reading skills. Nicky surprised you by completing many of the items well above his grade level and he announced, "This is kinda fun!" He scored at the high average level.

Questions for Students and Professionals

1 Does this test provide you with relevant information about how to help Nicky complete his nightly reading assignments?
2 Was the WJ-IV-ACH, a good choice of reading test to administer to Nicky? Why or why not?
3 Do you think his above average score is an accurate representation of his reading passage comprehension skills?
4 Think about the format of the WJ-IV-ACH, "Passage Comprehension" test. How might Nicky's performance be related to his ADHD?

Resources

American Educational Research Association: www.aera.net

American Psychological Association: www.apa.org/science/programs/testing/standards

Buros Center's Mental Measurements Yearbook (MMY) series: https://buros.org/mental-measurements-yearbook

Council For Exceptional Children (CEC): www.cec.sped.org

EBSCO: http://web.b.ebscohost.com.hnu.idm.oclc.org/

National Council on Measurement in Education: www.ncme.org/

Pearson Assessments: www.pearsonassessments.com

Pro Education, Inc.: www.proedinc.com/

Psychological Assessment Inc.: www.psychassessment.us/

Standards for Educational and Psychological Testing: www.apa.org/science/programs/testing/standards

WPS Publishing: www.wpspublish.com/store/p/2789/gort-5-gray-oral-reading-test-fifth-edition

Wrights Law: www.wrightslaw.com/

References

Association of Educational Therapists. (2016). Code of Ethics. Retrieved from www.aetonline.org/index.php/about/code-of-ethics

Association of Educational Therapists. (2017). Best Practices Exam Study Guide. Retrieved from www.aetonline.org/images/PDFs/BCET_Best_Practices_Exam_Study_Guide_5.2017.pdf

Blaustein, S. H. (2017). Test Review of the Comprehensive Test of Phonological Awareness, 2nd Edition. In J. F. Carlson, K. F. Geisinger & J. L. Jonson (Eds.), *The Mental Measurements Yearbook*. Lincoln, NE: Buros Center for Testing.

Canivez, G. (2017). Test Review of Woodcock–Johnson, 4th Edition. In J. F. Carlson, K. F. Geisinger & J. L. Jonson (Eds.), *The Mental Measurements Yearbook*. Lincoln, NE: Buros Center for Testing.

Carney, R. (2007). Test Review of RAN/RAS. In K. F. Geisinger, R. A. Spies, J. F. Carlson, & B. S. Plake (Eds.), *The Mental Measurements Yearbook*. Lincoln, NE: Buros Center for Testing.

36   Ethics and Foundational Practices

Castro-Villareal, F. (2017). Test Review of Test of Written Language, 4th Edition. In J. F. Carlson, K. F. Geisinger & J. L. Jonson (Eds.), *The Mental Measurements Yearbook*. Lincoln, NE: Buros Center for Testing.

Crehan, K. (2005). Test Review of the Test of Early Mathematical Ability, 3rd Edition. In R. A. Spies & B. S. Plake (Eds.), *The Mental Measurements Yearbook*. Lincoln, NE: Buros Center for Testing.

De Fur, S. (2017). Test Review of Test Early Written Language, 3rd Edition. In J. F. Carlson, K. F. Geisinger & J. L. Jonson (Eds.), *The Mental Measurements Yearbook*. Lincoln, NE: Buros Center for Testing.

Della-Piana, G. (2017). Test Review of Gray Oral Reading Test, 5th Edition. In J. F. Carlson, K. F. Geisinger & J. L. Jonson (Eds.), *The Mental Measurements Yearbook*. Lincoln, NE: Buros Center for Testing.

Engelhard, G. (2010). Test Review of Wide Range Achievement Test, 5th Edition. In R. A. Spies, J. F. Carlson & K. F. Geisinger (Eds.), *The Mental Measurements Yearbook*. Lincoln, NE: Buros Center for Testing.

Gross, T., (2017). Test Review of Test of Mathematical Ability, 3rd Edition. In J. F. Carlson, K. F. Geisinger & J. L. Jonson (Eds.), *The Mental Measurements Yearbook*. Lincoln, NE: Buros Center for Testing.

Hamilton, L. (2010). Test Review of Process Assessment of the Learner—Math, 2nd Edition. In R. A. Spies, J. F. Carlson & K. F. Geisinger (Eds.), *The Mental Measurements Yearbook*. Lincoln, NE: Buros Center for Testing.

Hammill, D. & Larsen, S. (2009). *Test of Written Language*, 4th edition (TOWL-4). Austin, TX: PRO-ED.

Harrison, G. (2017). Test Review of Test of Word reading Efficiency, 2nd Edition. In J. F. Carlson, K. F. Geisinger & J. L. Jonson (Eds.), *The Mental Measurements Yearbook*. Lincoln, NE: Buros Center for Testing.

Konold, T. & Blanchard, R. (2010). Test Review of Test of Auditory Perceptual Skills, 4th Edition. In R. A. Spies, J. F. Carlson & K. F. Geisinger (Eds.), *The Mental Measurements Yearbook*. Lincoln, NE: Buros Center for Testing.

Krach, S. (2010). Test Review of Process Assessment of the Learner, 2nd Edition. In R. A. Spies, J. F. Carlson & K. F. Geisinger (Eds.), *The Mental Measurements Yearbook*. Lincoln, NE: Buros Center for Testing.

Laughlin, G. (2010). Test Review of Key Math, 3rd Edition. In R. A. Spies, J. F. Carlson & K. F. Geisinger (Eds.), *The Mental Measurements Yearbook*. Lincoln, NE: Buros Center for Testing.

Marshall, M. & Matthaei, D. (2013). Guidelines for Conducting Standardized Assessment. *The Educational Therapist*, 34(1): 27–28.

McCurdy, M. & Hart, L. (2017). Test Review of Kaufman Test of Educational Achievement, 3rd Edition. In J. F. Carlson, K. F. Geisinger & J. L. Jonson (Eds.), *The Mental Measurements Yearbook*. Lincoln, NE: Buros Center for Testing.

McGrew, K. S., LaForte, E. M. & Schrank, F. A. (2014). *Woodcock–Johnson IV Technical Manual*. New York: Pearson Publishing.

Miller, M. (2010). Test Review of Wechsler Individual Achievement Test, 3rd Edition. In R. A. Spies, J. F. Carlson & K. F. Geisinger (Eds.), *The Mental Measurements Yearbook*. Lincoln, NE: Buros Center for Testing.

Moyle, M. J. (2016). Test Review of the Test of Integrated Language and Literacy Skills. In N. Nelson, E. Plante, N. Helm-Estabrooks & G. Hotz (Eds.), *The Mental Measurements Yearbook*. Lincoln, NE: Buros Center for Testing.

Neukrug, E. S. & Fawcett, R. C. (2009). *Essentials of Testing and Assessment: A Practical Guide for Counselors, Social workers, and Psychologists*, 2nd edition. Pacific Grove, CA: Brooks/Cole Publishing Co.

Poteat, M. G. (2007). Test Review of the Beery-Buktenica Developmental Test of Visual-Motor Integration, 6th Edition. In K. F. Geisinger, R. A. Spies, J. F. Carlson & B. S. Plake (Eds.), *The Mental Measurements Yearbook*. Lincoln, NE: Buros Center for Testing.

WIAT-III. (2009). *Wechsler Individual Achievement Test*, 3rd edition (WIAT-III). New York: Pearson.

Wiederholt, J. L. & Bryant, B. R. (2012). *GORT-5: Gray Oral Reading Tests, 5th Edition: Examiner's Manual*. Austin, TX: PRO-ED.

Table 2.2 Quick Reference to Reading Assessments

Name	Purpose	Ages/Grades	Areas of Assessment	Parallel Forms?	Author's Comments
GORT 5	Sequenced passages which are timed and read aloud followed by 5 comprehension questions.	Ages 6–23:11	Oral Reading, Rate, Accuracy, and Comprehension	2	Well-designed miscue marking system may help some to learn how to identify types of reading errors. Author always pairs GORT-5 with the WJ IV.
KTEA 3	Evaluates reading skills through a variety of measures.	Ages 4–25:11	Letter & Word Recognition, Nonword Decoding, Reading Comp., Decoding Fluency & Word Recognition Fluency (timed)	2	Often used by school districts for SPED. Services and annual IEP progress. A dyslexia screening test was published in 2014.
NDRT	Measures silent reading of HS and college students.	High school to 2- and 4-year colleges	Reading Vocab., Comprehension and Rate (all silent)	2	Author has no direct experience with the newest edition.
PAL II	Designed for measuring reading and writing skills and related processes.	Grades K–6	Phonological Decoding, Morphological Decoding, Silent Reading Fluency	No	Author has no direct experience with the test.
TOWRE 2	Measures the ability to pronounce printed words and phonemically regular nonwords accurately and fluently.	Ages 6–24:11	Sight Word Efficiency & Phonemic Decoding Efficiency (nonwords)	4	Author often pairs it with the WJ IV to determine if fluency training is indicated or if underlying skills are not yet established.

Table 2.2 (Cont.)

Name	Purpose	Ages/Grades	Areas of Assessment	Parallel Forms?	Author's Comments
WIAT-III	Designed to measure the achievement of students in prekindergarten through grade 12 in the areas of listening, speaking, reading, writing and mathematics.	Ages 4–50:11	Early Reading Skills, Reading Comprehension, Word Reading, Pseudoword Decoding, Oral Reading Fluency	No	Best used for understanding student performance on grade level school-based tasks. New dyslexia screener.
WJ-IV-ACH	Designed as part of norm-referenced tests for measuring intellectual abilities, academic achievement, and oral language abilities.	Ages 2–90+	Letter-Word Recognition, Sentence Reading Fluency, Passage Comp., Oral Reading, Reading Recall, Reading Vocab., Sound Awareness, Word Reading Fluency	3	Designed to be a diagnostic test. Understand that measuring each skill discretely usually yields a higher test score in each area. Passage comprehension is misnamed as the student doesn't read sustained text. Sound Awareness more like CTOPP-2.
WRAT-5	An achievement test battery designed to assess the core curricular domains of reading, mathematics, and oral and written language.	Ages 5–85+	Word Reading, Sentence Comprehension	2	Author does not use or recommend using this test as it has little diagnostic value.

Table 2.3 Quick Reference to Written Expression Assessments

Name	Purpose	Ages/Grades	Areas of assessment	Parallel Forms?	Author's Comments
KTEA-3	see Table 2.2	Ages 4–25:11	Writing Fluency, Written Expression, Spelling	2	Often used in public schools. Paired with K-ABC (Cognitive)
PAL II	see Table 2.2	Grades K–6	As per manual: assesses both productivity and quality in writing tasks	No	The links to evidence-based interventions can be very helpful.
TEWL-3	Measures understanding of language to construct a story and overall writing ability.	Ages 4–10:11	Basic Writing, Contextual Writing	2	Author no longer recommends using this test as scores are very inflated.
TILLS	TILLS is a comprehensive, norm-referenced test that has been standardized to identify oral and written language & literacy disorders	Ages 6–16	Oral and written language skills	No	Author has no direct experience with this instrument.
TOWL-4	Comprehensive test of written expression	Ages 9–17:11	Overall Writing, Contrived (dictated or directed), Spontaneous (using a picture to construct/write a story)	2	Comparison of subtest results yields useful information. Scores somewhat inflated.

Table 2.3 (Cont.)

Name	Purpose	Ages/Grades	Areas of assessment	Parallel Forms?	Author's Comments
WIAT-III	see Table 2.2	Grades K–12	Alphabet Writing Fluency, Spelling, Sentence Composition, Essay Composition	No	Best used for understanding student performance on grade level school-based tasks. Essay very difficult to score.
WJ-IV	see Table 2.2	Ages 2–90+	Writing Samples, Sentence Writing Fluency, Spelling, Spelling of Sounds, Editing	3	Designed to be a diagnostic test. Those who use it should understand that by measuring each skill discretely usually yields a higher test score in each area.
WRAT-5	see Table 2.2	Ages 5–85+	Spelling only	2	Limited use. Often used as a screening test in public schools.

Table 2.4 Quick Reference to Mathematics Assessments

Name	Purpose	Ages/Grades	Areas of assessment	Parallel Forms?	Author's Comments
KEY MATH 3	Measures many areas of math concepts and skills	Ages 4:6–21:11 Grades K-12	13 subtests incl: Basic Concepts, Numeration, Algebra, Geo., Meas., Operations, Written and Mental Comp., Estim.	2	Very comprehensive. Scoring now online. Essential Resources are very useful but at extra cost.
KTEA 3	Math part of a larger battery of academic skills. See Table 2.2.	Ages 4–25:11	Math Concepts and Applications, Math Comp., Math Fluency	2	Math aligns with Common Core. Author has no direct experience with this assessment.
PAL II M	Measures development of math cognitive processes and skills	Grades K–6	One assessment without subtests.	No	Very useful to understand why student is struggling, especially middle schoolers.
TEMA 3	Uses manipulatives to assess math skills and thinking.	Ages 3–8:11. Can be used with older students but not normed	One assessment without subtests	2	Attempts to measure the development of mathematical thinking. Separate purchase of probes and instructional activities is helpful.
TOMA 3	Can be used to identify students who are significantly behind their peers in math knowledge.	Ages 8:0–18:11	Mathematical Symbols and Concepts, Computation, Everyday Life, Word Probs., Attitude Toward Math	No	Author has no direct experience with this assessment.

Table 2.4 (Cont.)

Name	Purpose	Ages/Grades	Areas of assessment	Parallel Forms?	Author's Comments
WIAT III	Math subtests part of a larger battery of academic skills. See Table 2.2.	Grades K–12	Math Problem Solving, Numerical Operations, Math Fluency in Addition, Subtraction, Mult.	No	Untimed and timed portions. Measures school-based and grade level expectations.
WJ-IV-ACH	Math subtests part of a larger battery of academic skills. See Table 2.2.	Ages 2–90+	Applied Problems, Calculation, Math Facts Fluency, Number Matrices	3	Designed to be a diagnostic test. Understand that measuring each skill discretely usually yields a higher test score in each area.
WRAT 5	Math subtests part of a larger battery of academic skills. See Table 2.2.	Ages 5–85+	Math Computation only	2	Time limit on written math problems. Not recommended by this author for anything more than screening.

Table 2.5 Quick Reference to Processing Assessments

Name	Purpose	Ages/Grades	Areas of assessment	Parallel Forms?	Author's Comments
Beery VMI-6	Measures Visual-Motor Integration skills.	Short Form: 2–7Full Form: 8+	No subtests used	No	Best to use Full Form as most younger children "ceiling out" on Short Form. Manual supports understanding how VMI skills typically develop.
CTOPP-2	Evaluates phonological processing abilities including rapid naming and memory.	Test for Ages 4–6, another for 7–24	Elision, Blending Words, Sound Matching, Phoneme Isolation, Blending Nonwords, Memory for Digits, Rapid Letter Naming, Rapid Color Naming, Rapid Object Naming	No	CTOPP-2 very effective as a part of dyslexia screening.Uses a CD for portions of the test.
RAN/RAS	Quick assessment of rapid naming speed.	Ages 5:0–18:11	Rapid Automatized Naming and Rapid Alternating Stimulus	No	An effective measure of rapid naming.
TAPS -4	Measures language processing in 3 areas: phonological, auditory memory, and listening comprehension.	Ages 5–21	Phonological Processing = Word (Pair) Discrimin., Phon. Deletion, Phon. Blending, Syllabic Blending	No	Very useful screening tool for Lang. Processing. Uses a CD for portions of the test. Subtest has ability to measure following oral directions when background noise present.

3 The Basics of Psychometrics Explained

Introduction

Whether you are scoring an assessment you have just completed or are interpreting test scores that have been sent to you, it is important to know what the scores mean. All assessments use similar terminology that, while common to people in the psychometric field, can be confusing to others not trained in the subject. Further, some terms have been used incorrectly over time and confuse the issue. This chapter is designed to:

1 demystify the world of psychometry (in fact, that term will be used very little after this);
2 define the terms that are commonly used; and
3 make interpretation of these terms (and the scores associated with them) simpler to understand so that you may use them with confidence to as you work to understand the data.

"Rachel" has asked her local public school to assess her 6th-grade daughter's math skills. "Cassie" attends a "progressive" K–8th-grade independent school and does not enjoy math. At Rachel's request, she has just received a brief summary of the scores in advance of the school meeting scheduled for next week. She has ascertained that Cassie has above average intelligence and was attentive while attempting all of the math tasks on the WJ-IV-ACH but sometimes "balked" at completing some sections. According to Rachel, Cassie enjoys reading and prefers playing her drums over doing math homework. Rachel says Cassie's drumming sounds more like "rhythmic banging" but she always seems so happy after drumming. Lately, Cassie has expressed an interest in joining the middle school's robotic club.

With math demands increasing in the 6th grade, Rachel wants to be certain Cassie will receive all the math support she needs. Rachel has engaged you to be Cassie's educational therapist (ET) as you are comfortable remediating math issues. She has asked you to review the standard scores and help her make sense of them. Can you do this with certainty? If not, this chapter should be very helpful.

46　The Basics of Psychometrics Explained

The scores also list something called "Confidence Level." What is that? Rachel wants to know if that is a measure of how confident "Cassie" appeared when approaching the different types of math tasks. Is it? Read on, if you are not sure how to answer Rachel.

Assessment follows a meaningful and purposeful sequence of events:

1　*choose* the instrument(s) to answer referral questions;
2　*administer* the test(s) correctly;
3　*score* the test(s) correctly;
4　*analyze* the resulting scores within each test and between all tests administered;
5　spend time to *interpret* and create an understanding of what the scores mean; and
6　make *recommendations* based on your findings.

Think of this sequence as a *cascade* of events (see Figure 3.1). *Any* error along this sequence can compromise or nullify your work. Without accurate raw scores and correct determination of the student's age, the results are meaningless and any derived analysis based on these faults will negate your interpretation.

Avoid Common Errors

One common error is incorrectly determining the student's chronological age. Since it is "best practice" to determine scores based on the student's chronological age, rather than grade level, it is critical to determine that correctly. Once I used the student's birthdate listed on the developmental history form which had been completed by his mother. The computer derived scores did not match my impressions of how the student actually performed when conducting the assessments. So, I calculated the age "by hand." Now, the student appeared to be two years older than he should be! I asked the mother about his date of birth. She had listed his brother's date of birth by accident! Now, I always ask the student how old s/he is before beginning any assessments as a "quick check" prior to formally calculating the chronological age for scoring purposes. (Nearly every child knows how old s/he is!) Many assessments can be scored online. That still requires inputting a correct date of birth. It is best to know how to accurately calculate the chronological age of the examinee. Remember, if one miscalculates the chronological age, *all* the scoring will be in error. There are many helpful (and free) chronological age calculators available online (e.g. www.thecalculator.co/time/Chronological-Age-Calculator-288.html).

A second common area for those scoring "by hand" is using the wrong table. It is quite easy to read a raw score off the wrong table or from an incorrect line on the appropriate table. It can be very helpful to use ruler or side of a file folder to help you read across from the raw score to the standard score. If you are using computer scoring, this will be less of an issue but it is

The Basics of Psychometrics Explained 47

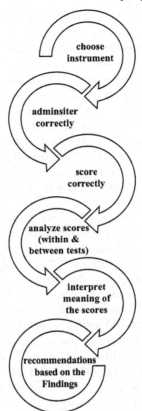

Figure 3.1 Assessment Cascade

still possible to make an error in transferring numbers from the test protocol (completed test record form) or by mistyping them.

Based in my many years instructing graduate students in assessment and supervising others, another common scoring mistake is to miscount the raw score. Always verify the raw scores *before* looking them up on the scoring chart or inputting in the computerized scoring. Although a raw score, in itself, tells you almost nothing about how the student performed, it is *essential* to count each correctly. Using an incorrect raw score creates a *domino effect* of erroneous work. If the resulting score determination is inflated or deflated, your analysis and interpretation of the data will be flawed and your *report of findings* (see Chapters 5 and 6) will be seriously compromised. Any recommendations or resulting treatment plan will be incorrect in possibly egregious ways. As noted in the previous example, keeping track of the student performance on grade level tasks is very helpful. If your subsequent scoring indicates that the student's standard score is average or higher and you noted s/he was struggling - something is clearly wrong.

48 *The Basics of Psychometrics Explained*

Some may feel overly confident that the derived scores are correct when using computer-generated scoring, which does not require "looking up" scores. However, if you did not determine the raw score correctly and entered an erroneous one, the computer scoring cannot know the raw score is incorrect. It is important to remember that, for many of the standardized instruments, once the *basal* is established one counts the items above (before) the first item you actually administered, as *also* being correct. If one does not "count in" the items before the basal as being correct, the resulting score may be seriously diminished, indicating that the student has much lower skills than is the case. This may potentially skew the results, your analysis, interpretation and recommendations. Check the examiner's manual to verify the basal rules which apply to each test, as you determine the raw score.

It is *nearly always* best practice to score based on the student's chronological age. This is important because students may be nearly a year younger or older in a grade, based on their age upon entering school. (Think of the age range differences in kindergarteners.) Processing tests are very sensitive to developmental and age ranges. Use the student's chronological age, even if a test gives you an option to use the grade level to produce scores. Chronological ages are written giving both the age and month using a hyphen or colon. So, a 9-year-4-month-old boy's chronological age would be written as 9–4 or 9:4. A young woman who has just celebrated her 17th birthday would have her chronological age written as 17–0 or 17:0. Chronological ages *are not* ever written using a period. The period signifies the grade level and month in the school year of that grade. 9.4 would indicate that the boy is in the 9th grade and he is in the 4th month of school (or December of that school year). I have reviewed many student reports where age and grade level both use the period (e.g. 7.2). Wait! Is the student seven years old or in the 7th grade? Do not confuse and miswrite chronological age and/or grade level notations. This is a clear way to signal to others that you are not a skilled assessor.

However, there is one instance where one *should not* use chronological age to score. If the student has been "retained" or "held out" a year, for any reason, s/he would be older than their peers. In that case, s/he would not have been exposed to the same curriculum and would not have had the opportunity to learn many of the academic skills as their age-peers. The *Essentials of the WIAT-III and KTEA-II Assessment* explains:

> when a student has been retained in a grade, comparing him or her to age-mates assumes that the equivalent instructional opportunity has been provided. In such a case, the individual might have lower scores because some skills have not been taught. For this reason, grade-based scores are typically preferred …

(Lichtenberger & Breaux 2010: 65)

The Basics of Psychometrics Explained 49

Table 3.1 Commonly Used Terms in Standardized Assessment

Term	Definition
Achievement	Previous learning.
Percentile Rank	The percentage of people or scores that occur at or below a given score.
Reliability	The extent to which a score or measure is free of measurement error. This ratio can be estimated using a variety of computational measures (for example: test-retest and parallel forms). A test's reliability will be stated in the Technical or Examiner's manual. The *Mental Measurements Yearbook* (see Chapter 2) also discusses this aspect of each test.
Scaled Scores	Scaled Scores have a mean of 10 and a standard deviation of 3. Scaled Scores are commonly used for subtests especially on cognitive tests.
Standard Error of Measurement	An index of the amount of error in a test or measure. A measure is most accurate when the standard error is small. The amount of error is stated in the Examiner's manual and may also be displayed in the test report such as is shown in Figure 3.4.
Standard Score	Standard Scores are a reliable way to compare student's performance on different tests and from one year to another. The most common standard score has a mean of 100 and a standard deviation of 15.
Validity	The extent to which a test measures the quality it purports to measure. Types of validity evidence include content validity, criterion validity, and construct validity evidence. Again, one can consult the MMY for a review of a test's validity.

Source: Definitions from Psychological Testing: Principles, Applications, and Issues 7th Edition (Kaplan & Saccuzzo, 2009).

Should I Use Age or Grade Equivalent Scores?

The simple and emphatic answer is "No!" As simple as they seem, these two measures of student achievement are full of misconceptions and misunderstandings. Neither is what its name implies and they are both unhelpful in understanding a student's profile. Some school districts routinely only report these types of scores. These districts have explained to the author that those scores make the most sense to parents. However, they are not accurate and should *not* be used. Both of these equivalent scores mislead educators and parents into thinking that a student is operating at a certain age level or grade

50   *The Basics of Psychometrics Explained*

level. This is not true and cannot be determined with the sampling method that standardized tests use. It takes a criterion-referenced or other skills-based assessment to determine what a student has/has not mastered at a certain grade level (or age). When a grade equivalent score indicates a 4th grader is operating at the "12th grade level" in reading, that does not mean that the student would be successful if placed in a 12th grade English class. Similarly, a reading age-level equivalent score of 17 would not mean that the 4th grader reads as well as a 17-year-old, nor would the 4th grader be able to read material at that level.

Further, age and grade equivalents are not a ratio or interval scale of measurement. They cannot be added, subtracted, or averaged. Using age equivalents and grade equivalents has been advised against by the International Reading Association, the American Research Association, the American Psychological Association and the National Council on Measurement in Education.

What Measurement Should I Use Instead?

Standardized tests produce two types of data that allow you to make comparisons: standard scores and percentile ranks. Use the standard score or the associated percentile rank, which shows where the student is performing relative to his/her peers. Standard scores can be compared and summarized: "Standard scores are a more accurate representation of a student's skill levels because they are based not only on the mean at a given age level but also on the distribution of scores" (Pearson Assessments undated). Table 3.1 shows some commonly used terms in standardized assessment.

About Percentile Ranks

Percentile ranks are commonly reported and are often coupled with the standard score. What is a percentile rank? An easily understood definition of a percentile rank is the number where a certain percentage of scores are equal to or fall below that number. To begin to understand this concept, think of rank as being a line or queue. Imagine lining up to buy tickets to a very limited event where only 100 people will be able to buy tickets. There are 100 people in line and counting begins at the back of the line. You are in the 53rd slot. Your friend arrived very early this morning and is in the 89th slot. Thinking of a percentile rank, you are at the 53rd percentile rank with 47 people behind you. Your friend is in the 89th rank with 88 people behind her. There are only 11 people in front of her in this ticket line. She is likely to be able to purchase really good seats!

Since tests are normed by having thousands of people taking the same test to create the normal distribution, there will be many, many people whose scores fall on the same data point. Percentiles range from.01 percent to 99.9 percent. Then, "a percentile rank is the percentage of people of the examinee's age, who have the examinee's score or lower" (Schneider et al. 2018: 150). It does *not* refer to the percentage of items correct. If your score is at the 90th percentile, that means you scored as well as or better than 90% of people who took the test. There are not many who did better than you and many, many others who did less well than you.

Standard Scores differ from percentile ranks because they have equal intervals, whereas percentile ranks do not (Schneider et al. 2018: 146). It is fine to report scores in percentiles, but it good to train yourself to think about comparing test results in standard scores, as well. One can always use a Standard Score to Percentile Conversion table to quickly "translate" a standard score into *percentile rank* and to learn to recognize the relative value of each standard score. Standard Score to Percentile Conversion tables are readily found online and in the back of many assessment manuals (for example see www.wrightslaw.com/advoc/articles/sscore.table.pdf).

Using a Standard Score to Percentile Conversion Chart, can you find the percentile ranks and describe how "Cassie" did on the WJ-IV-ACH measures of math?

Subtest Name	Standard Score	Percentile Rank
Applied Problems	87	
Calculations	86	
Math Fact Fluency	78	
Number Matrices	81	

When you have done an assessment using a standardized (or "normed") test or tests, you need to convert the student's actual ("raw") score into a score that will allow you to use it for comparison purposes. You want to know where that raw score places the student amongst his/her peers. To do this, one must convert the raw scores to a "Standard" Score, (SS); that places the score on a "normal" distribution among other possible test scores for that assessment. A normal distribution is what many call a normal "curve" or "bell curve" due to its shape. The bell curve is a graph whose shape depends on two factors- the mean and the standard deviation. The mean is the position of the center and the deviation determines height and width of the bell shape.

Standard Deviation

This term tends to make some anxious when they hear it thinking that it is calculated from some kind of wildly complex formula. And, if you see the formula set out in a math or statistics book, you might agree. Actually, all you need to know about standard deviation (SD) is that it is a measure of how far data vary (deviate) from the mean (average). Think of it as an average of the data's distance from the mean. When tests are standardized, and many, many

52 *The Basics of Psychometrics Explained*

people take the test to produce the standard deviation, their scores create a normal curve around the mean. The standard deviation is based on the raw scores' differences from the mean. Fortunately, when using any standardized assessments, you are never required to calculate the SD, because that has already been done. But you need to understand the meaning of standard deviation (see Figure 3.2).

Quick Facts

In a normal distribution:

- The total area under the curve is 100%
- About 68% of the area under the curve falls within ±1 standard deviation
- About 95% of the area under the curve falls within ±2 standard deviations
- About 99.7 of the area under the curve falls within ±3 standard deviations
- The distribution is concentrated in the center and decreases on either side.
- The data has less of a tendency to produce extreme values.(Russell 2019)

How Test Scores Are Derived

Test score theory is based on the notion that, given a large enough population that takes the test, people's scores will arrange themselves along a normal curve. As you can see from Figure 3.2, there are many more scores in the "middle" of the curve than at the ends. Also, notice also the symmetry of the curve. 50% of the scores are to the left of the "middle"; 50 % to the right; and as scores move from the center, the number of scores in those ranges, drops off rapidly to near zero at each end. Almost no one scores in those ranges, which is why those scoring in those ranges are sometimes called "outliers."

To use an example familiar to most, the SAT test (Math, Verbal, or Writing) is a standardized test that has a range of 200–800, a mean of 500 and a standard deviation of 100, making it relatively easy to use. From the illustration below, you can see that about 68% of the test-takers will fall between 500 ± 100 points or 400–600. Ninety-six percent of the scores will be between 500 ± 200 points or 300–700. Anyone who scores over 700 would be in a very elite group, representing the top 2% (or better) of test takers.

Although the Federal Law, IDEA Part B, §300.8(c) (10) no longer requires using the discrepancy formula to determine eligibility, in many states, eligibility for special education services is still based on the discrepancy model (see American Speech-Language-Hearing Association undated). The difference between the ability (usually measured by a cognitive test) and a standardized achievement, such as the WIAT-III or WJ-IV-ACH (see Chapter 2) is calculated. If the discrepancy (difference) between the two standard scores is at least 1.5 SD and a deficit in processing skills is documented, the student will likely qualify for special education services.

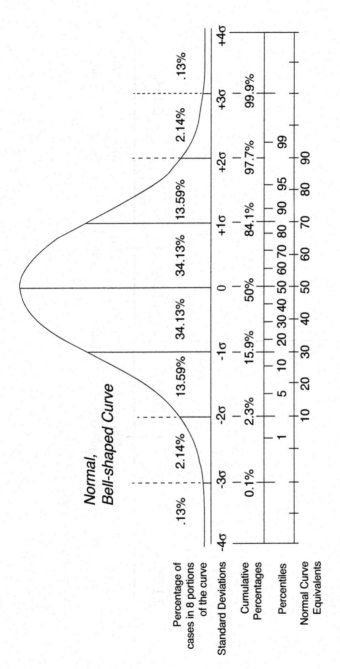

Figure 3.2 The Bell-shaped Curve
Adapted from www.parinc.com

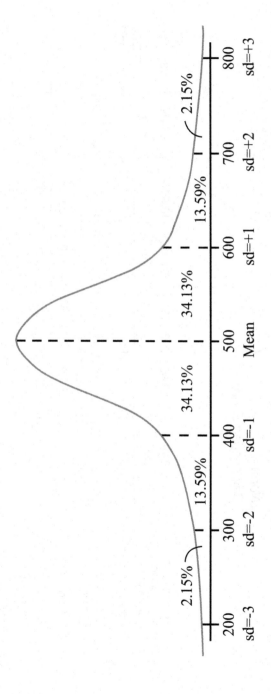

Figure 3.3 Normal Distribution SAT Scores

Z-scores

Scores that are reported in terms of standard deviations are known as Z-scores. A Z-score indicates how far the score is from the mean in standard deviations. For example, a Z-score of +1.0 means the student scored one SD above the mean, about the 84th percentile. Where did that number come from? To answer that, look back at the Figure 3.2 and note that 50 + 34 = 84%. To use another example, a Z-score of –1.0 would translate to the 16th percentile rank (50 – 34 = 16).

More than likely, the test maker will not use these Z-scores but will have converted them to "standard scores" with a different scale, like the SAT does. Given the earlier SAT example, the 600 score would be generated from a +1.0 Z-score. Suffice it to say that this can seem confusing if every test uses a different scale though many use a scale similar to cognitive (IQ) tests, which have a mean of 100 and an SD of 15. It is interesting to note that "Standard" scores are not really standard. The reason is the word, as it is used here, refers to "standardizing" the scores, not that they all use the same scale. In fact, the definition of "standard score" is what is called the Z-score here. This is why using percentile ranks can help you with comparing results across tests and most readers are used to thinking about and comparing results using percentile ranks. While the "standard score" scales may vary, the percentiles can be compared directly. Just be clear when explaining the assessment results to parents to clarify the difference between *percentile rank* and *percentage correct*. See Chapter 6 to learn how to explain tests results to parents and avoid this potential misunderstanding, and see Wright and Darr Wright (2016) for a detailed, carefully constructed and "parent friendly" explanation of the psychometrics of assessment scores is on: www.wrightslaw.com/advoc/articles/tests_measurements.html

Remember that, while you need to know how the scores are derived, you will not be required to calculate them. The scores will be accessed in a table in the examiner's manual or, if the test scoring is computer-based, from the data file in the computer. They will be accurate if you are using a well-constructed and technically reliable instrument, have computed the chronological age correctly, and have calculated the raw scores (or composite scores based on the raw scores) accurately. What matters is that you understand what the scores mean.

Interpreting the Scores

The value of any assessment instrument is what it tells you about the student. There should be many factors in analyzing a student's strengths and weaknesses. Assessment scores are just one piece of the puzzle. If you have done an assessment or are given assessment results to evaluate, it is important to know what the scores mean and what they can or cannot tell you.

56   *The Basics of Psychometrics Explained*

Test scores are only as good as the test from which they came. Some tests are very accurate and others are not as good. The term used in testing is *reliable*. Reliability is the extent to which a score or measure is free of measurement error. "Theoretically, reliability is the ratio of true score variance to observed score variance. This ratio can be estimated using a variety of correlational methods, including coefficient alpha, Kuder-Richardson 20, test–retest and parallel forms" (Kaplan & Saccuzzo 2009: 620). It is critical to use tests with a reliability of 80% or better, as that is considered fairly reliable. Tests with 90% reliability (or better) are considered very reliable. Consider reliability in choosing what tests to purchase and use.

Test–retest reliability measures whether there is consistency in the test results when the test is given on different occasions. *Parallel forms* reliability indicates whether scores would be very similar when using the different forms of the same test such as the GORT-3 Form A and B. Several years ago, the MMY reviewers had criticized some of the technical aspects of an earlier version of this test. In particular, there was criticism about the documentation of the equivalency of Forms A and B (Crumpton & Miller-Whitehead 2003). Previously, ET colleagues and I had noted and shared among ourselves that Form B scored a student much *lower* than Form A. To check this, I had used both forms with the same student one week apart. Indeed, Form B scored her significantly lower. Imagine if I had used Form A to originally measure "Caitlin's" reading skills and after working with her for nine months and observing good progress, had retested using her using Form B in preparation for a progress report meeting. Consider the dismay and consternation of her parents hearing that Caitlin's reading had declined! I can just hear, "Why have we been spending all that money time, and effort to improve her reading?" Of course, the true issue would have been the lack of reliable parallel forms. The technical issues report in the MMY regarding the revised GORT-4 stated that the issue with parallel forms was addressed. Each test has its reliability listed in the technical manual. It is something to research and seriously consider *before* purchasing and using an assessment instrument. If the reliability is low, what are you actually measuring and how valid are the scores you are reporting?

Standard Error of Measurement

For each standardized test, its scores and the subtest scores have a "Standard Error of Measurement" (SEM). This allows one to estimate the degree to which a test provides an accurate measure of the skills being assessed. The larger the standard error of measurement, the less certain you can be about the accuracy of the aspect being measured. If a test is highly reliable, the standard error will be low. When reliability reduces, standard error increases.

Standard error is usually reported in the technical manual as a range of plus or minus amount of percentile rank. To help understand this important

The Basics of Psychometrics Explained 57

concept, think of polling a group. When a poll reports the number of people who in favor of or are against something, the result is always couched with a "margin of error" of so many percentage points. It is the same for Standard of Error of Measurement. If a test has a standard error of + 2 or -2 and the student's score is at the 25th percentile, the actual score could range anywhere between the 23rd to 27th percentile. Although we may confidently report a SS of 110 (or 74%), that is not the true score. If that test/subtest has a standard error of 5, the true SS score could fall anywhere between 105–115. This calculation gives a range where the student likely would have scored with 80 to 90% confidence. One can think of these ranges as bands of scores. Tests scored by computers often show this using a shaded band on a scale from 0 to 100%. See the sample report on the Key Math-3 provided by the publisher (Figure 3.4). Remember, the less reliable the test, the larger the range will be and "your ability to make precise statements is greatly diminished" (Kaplan & Saccuzzo 2009: 125). Kaplan and Saccuzzo add:

> Perhaps the most useful index for reliability for the interpretation of individual scores is the standard error of measurement. This index is used to create an interval around an observed score. The wider the interval, the lower the reliability of the score. Using the standard error measurement, we can say that we are 95% confident that a person's true score falls between two values.
>
> (Kaplan & Saccuzzo 2009: 125)

Confidence Level or Confidence Intervals

Test publishers compute confidence levels or confidence intervals (CI) using internal consistency which tends to be higher than test–retest reliability (Schneider et al. 2018: 274). Simply stated, it is related to standard error of measurement. It is a measure of how likely it is that the reported score falls within a certain interval or band, described in the example of the Key Math-3 (Figure 3.4). Common intervals used are the 68% interval, the 95% interval and the 99% interval. For some of the comprehensive academic tests of achievement that are scored using computer software, you will be asked to choose the confidence level. At the 68% interval, there is a probability of 68 percent that the student's derived score is actually *in* that range. At the 95% interval, there is a probability of 95 percent that the student's derived score is actually in that range and that range (or band) will be much larger. It can be very instructive to use the raw score and first choose the 68% interval, to calculate the score and band. Next, choose the 95% interval, to calculate the score and band. Compare the difference. What band is larger? Importantly, now can you answer Rachel's question about whether the WJ-IV-ACH reported confidence level measures how confident "Cassie" appeared when performing different math tasks?

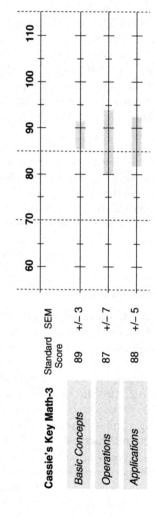

Figure 3.4 SEM Confidence Band

Reminders

Because we are often reporting assessment results that may have significance in the life of the student, using reliable assessment instruments and understanding what the scores mean is essential.

Whether one is given scores from another professional or assessed the student yourself, the key to all of this is the interpretation of the results (see Chapter 4). What does the information tell you about the student? What does it *not* tell you? What scores seem to be pointing in the same direction, likely confirming a strength or weakness? Which scores were unexpected and become a puzzle to be hypothesized about, explored and analyzed? To do this well, one must understand what the instrument does or does not measure, how it measures the skill area and whether it is considered reliable (see Chapter 2 for the MMY reviews).

Summary

If you are giving an assessment, read/review the examiner's manual for pertinent information such as establishing a basal (floor), determining a ceiling (how many items must be incorrect before you stop testing), and scoring system (whether some items worth more than others). Be certain that you have at the ready all of the materials that are needed. If there is timing involved, have a clock/phone nearby. Scores obtained from these assessments are only as good as the examiner's appropriate administration of that measure.

Determining a score is based on two important items: the *student's age* and *raw score*. If either of these is miscalculated, the results will not be valid. Calculate the age carefully to be sure you have the correct years *and* months. Does the number seem right? How old did the student say s/he is? In computing the raw score, it is essential to know the correct procedure. Do you count items before the basal as correct? How is the ceiling determined? Do certain items have different point values or variable points? How do you score items the student "skipped"? The raw score will determine what the standard score and percentile rank will be so accuracy is critical. Lastly, if you are using tables to look up the scores, be sure you have the correct table and are on the correct line. Double check *everything* before scoring. Reporting assessment results (or interpreting those given by others) may have significant importance, so understanding what the scores mean is a professional responsibility for all ETs.

Practice understanding standardized scores by answering the following questions regarding Cassie's scores and those on a sample KeyMath-3 report.

Self-review Questions for Students and Professionals

1   Do you feel more confident in your understanding of standard scores? If specific questions remain, how can you find the answers?
2   Cassie was tested in October and is in the 6th grade. How should you write her current grade level?

60 *The Basics of Psychometrics Explained*

3 Cassie is eleven years old and four months. Use the proper notation to write that.
4 Use a standard score to percentile rank conversion table to find "Cassie's" associated percentile ranks.

WJ-IV-ACH Test Name	Standard Score	Percentile Rank
Applied Problems	87	
Calculations	86	
Math Fact Fluency	78	
Number Matrices	81	

1 Which (if any) of the above scores fall within the average range?
2 Define Standard Error of Measurement.
3 On most scales, *average* standard scores range from 85 to 115. Using the confidence interval (CI) on the Key Math-3 or WJ-IV-ACH, would any of the score descriptors change from *average* to *below average*?
4 Do the scores make clear why Cassie is struggling with math? (If not, see Chapter 4.)

Questions for Parents

1 Do you have a better understanding of what the standardized tests scores for your child mean?
2 Can you explain the difference between a percentile rank and a percentage correct?
3 Have you accessed (or plan to access) the online assessment article from Wright's Law designed for parents?
4 If you have been given *only* grade equivalent or age equivalent scores for your child, are you prepared to advocate by asking for the standard scores or percentile ranks?
5 Can you use a conversion table to "translate" standard scores to percentile rank scores?

Acknowledgement

The author thanks Geoffrey D. Underwood for his assistance in the preparation of this chapter.

Resources

Psychological Assessment Resources: www.parinc.com

Weiss, L. G. (2018). *Standardized Assessment for Clinical Practitioners: A Primer*. New York: Pearson.

References

American Speech-Language-Hearing Association. (Undated). IDEA Part B Issue Brief: Identification of Specific Learning Disabilities. Retrieved from www.asha.org/Advocacy/federal/idea/IDEA-Part-B-Issue-Brief-Identification-of-Specific-Learning-Disabilities

Crumpton, N. L. & Miller-Whitehead, M., (2003). Test Review of Gray Oral Reading Test, 4th Edition. In B. S. Plake, J. C. Impara & R. A. Spies (Eds.), *The Mental Measurements Yearbook*. Lincoln, NE: Buros Center for Testing.

Kaplan, R. M. & Saccuzzo, D. P. (2009). *Psychological Testing: Principles, Applications, and Issues 7th Edition*. Belmont, CA: Wadsworth Cengage Learning.

Lichtenberger, E. O. & Breaux, K. (2010). *Essentials of WIAT-III and KTEA-2 Assessment*. Hoboken, NJ: John Wiley & Sons.

Pearson Assessments. (Undated). Interpretation Problems of Age and Grade Equivalent. Retrieved from www.pearsonassessments.com/campaign/interpretation-problems-of-age-and-grade-equivalents.html

Russell, D. (2019). Bell Curve and Normal Distribution Definition. Retrieved from www.thoughtco.com/bell-curve-normal-distribution-defined-2312350

Schneider, J. W., Lichtenberger, E. O., Mather, N. & Kaufman, N. L. (2018). *Essentials of Assessment Report Writing*, 2nd edition. Hoboken, NJ: John Wiley & Sons.

Wright, P. and Darr Wright, P. (2016). Tests and Measurements for the Parent, Teacher, Advocate & Attorney. Retrieved from www.wrightslaw.com/advoc/articles/tests_measurements.html

4 Creating the Student's Profile

Introduction

In this chapter you will learn how to construct the student's academic profile using the test data, observations of the student's approach to tasks during the assessment, his/her affect, comments, level of engagement and persistence, along with the test format and construction. These all need to be integrated. None are sufficient by themselves to gain a nuanced understanding of the student's strengths and weaknesses. Chapter 4 explains my "constellation approach" that uses a group of questions, attributes and/or descriptors to create working hypotheses which may be tested during the assessment process. Hypothesis testing, along with actual test results, are critical to determining different types of learning issues and to create an accurate *learner's profile*.

What if there is No Problem?

In private practice, you will not be assessing unless you have already been contacted by a parent who has sought assessment or you are assessing to establish baseline data for a new or existing client. However, as a school-based educational therapist, there may be times when you are tasked with assessing a student but the parent is not ready to agree. Remember Ben from Chapter 1? He was not really ready to have his child assessed. If a parent does not recognize that there is an issue, no number of "compelling" tests scores are going to be persuasive. Or, one parent may be concerned but the other does not yet acknowledge or "see" the issue. Frankly, it is not wise to rush into assessment without some level of "buy in." The agreement could be as limited as, "Her mother thinks there is an issue so I am willing to have it looked into." Or, "Since the teacher is concerned, I guess we should be, too." But how do you proceed until then? Are there techniques that might move the parent(s) to agreement?

There are three basic approaches. First, you engage in a dialogue. Those conversations may take place at regular intervals across weeks or months in a private practice before there is movement. I recall such a conversation where the father crossed his arms somewhat defensively and said, "He sounds just like

Creating the Student's Profile 63

me at his age ... and I turned out just fine!" The response would be to say, "That is great, but 'Tony' may not have your resiliency. And the issue may not be *exactly* like yours and resolve itself." However, in Tony's case, his mother intervened and said very lovingly and respectfully, "You did turn out to be a terrific man. But, if you are honest with yourself, you didn't get to do *everything* you wanted in life because your learning issues got in the way. Don't you want Tony to have *all* the career options open to him?"

In an independent school setting, there may be no movement towards assessment for years. In cases like these, careful documentation in school progress reports is essential. I have heard a parent exclaim angrily, "Why are we just hearing about this now? How can Jenny be so far behind and we never knew about it?" Then I could answer, "Actually, there are comments recorded every year since the first grade. But since you are aware of it now, let us find out how to help Jenny."

And, some parents wait rather than agreeing to assessment when the issue is first raised because they feel that "maturation" will take care of the problem. That assertion is fairly easy to counter since most of the assessment instruments that measure different types of cognitive processing are based on developmental constructs (see Chapter 2). In other words, if Jenny measures very low on her visual memory, visual motor integration, or phonological processing skills, she is being compared to others her same age. If she scores at the 10th percentile rank compared to her peers, it is not "developmental" and without appropriate intervention she is not going to suddenly "bloom."

Respectful dialogue with the parents is always a good first course of action. Another approach is to ask the student how school and/or learning is going for them. Since schools are social environments, students readily compare themselves to others. *Everyone else seems to be able to do this. Why can't I?* Every student that I have assessed knows that learning is not going well for her/him in *some* regard and this can be conveyed to the parents. In the public school setting, I assessed as a part of a special education team. There, I assessed students as young as kindergarten (5 or 6 years old). I recall one kindergartener telling me, "I can learn stuff. I just can't remember it!" And, he was absolutely correct. He had significant issues with memory and recall. Often, the student has expressed a sense of relief about being assessed because it signals that adults have noticed the student's distress. If one is able to gently inquire or watch for signs of frustration, many students readily reveal their struggles and are hoping for meaningful support.

Lastly, if the parents are not defensive but truly do not see the issue, I assign some "homework," if they are willing. Each task is designed to enable the parent(s) to view the student's struggles first hand. For example, I recall a girl who read well but did not understand what she was reading. The parents were astounded that the school had a concern. They had heard "Lucy" read aloud quite fluently so assumed she was comprehending everything she could read. I asked the mother to take turns reading aloud from a "chapter book" her daughter was currently reading at night. I requested that she ask Lucy to

64 *Creating the Student's Profile*

summarize after reading the chapter aloud. Lucy's mom reported in after a week, saying that summarizing was "Kinda hard for Lucy" but she was not convinced there was an issue. I thanked her and suggested that during the following week of reading aloud, she ask Lucy to recall the main idea and specific details. Lucy's mom called again to tell me that Lucy could generally recall some details but not really state the main idea. She was now sounding a bit worried but not certain any action was necessary. I asked her to read with Lucy for one more week and determine if Lucy could recall a sequence of events. When she called at the end of the week, she said Lucy could *not* recall a sequence of events accurately and could *not* anticipate what might happen next, although this was an action-packed book. Lucy's mom was growing more alarmed and asked what could be done about this? Time to assess.

Asking Questions to Create a Working Hypothesis

As stated in Chapter 1, asking relevant questions is the key to formulating a working hypothesis about what might be the underpinnings of area(s) of concern. Assessment begins with the clinical interview and the process of gathering information. The ET asks questions of parents, reads teacher reports or written comments, and examines current work samples. Then, the ET thinks about the probable causes of a student's lack of progress toward reaching expectations and designs an assessment plan that will confirm or "rule out" the suspected causes.

Many non-LD possibilities exist: the student may not have had adequate exposure to the materials, or insufficient practice; attendance may have been spotty due to health issues or frequent moves; the pace of instruction may have been too brisk or the curriculum too accelerated; or perhaps there has been a "spiraling curriculum," which assumes that prior concepts are mastered and ready to be built upon. The ET does not first assume there is a learning difference, but considers alternative explanations, such as issues with attention, emotional distress, or self-regulation difficulties so the student wasn't "available for instruction" although physically present. An ET can support academic development for any of these circumstances without conducting a significant amount of formal assessment.

Constellations

When non-LD issues are ruled out, the ET begins to think of "constellations" or clusters of issues that often underscore each type of LD. Like a physician, the ET asks questions, looks at work samples, and listens to the descriptions provided by those who know the student best—parents, teachers, and, if s/he is older, the student or client. These descriptors "rule in" or "rule out" possible hypotheses. By forming questions and engaging in hypothesis testing, one creates an assessment plan. For example: The fifth-grade student is clumsy, lacking in social skills, has a good vocabulary possibly suggesting a determination of Nonverbal Learning Disability (NVLD). However, if he has strong skills in math and visual-spatial thinking, that possibility is ruled out, so another hypothesis must be created for having limited social skills and "clumsiness" (all concerns) accompanied by strengths in vocabulary, math and visual-spatial skills. Do you see that the emphasis has shifted? More questions need to be asked and more pre-assessment data needs to be gathered.

Thinking clinically and diagnostically about "constellations" of reported strengths and weaknesses helps to develop an assessment plan. I use the term *constellation* like one might view a star pattern in the night sky. It is a collection and arrangements of stars that together create a recognizable pattern. It does not need to be a linear progression, rather a grouping that creates an observable and discernable pattern. It is the goal of an evaluation to create a working hypothesis about why the student is struggling or not achieving as expected. Do not be discouraged by "ruling out" some possibilities for learning issues. Verifying, refining, adding to or disproving the original hypothesis is a valid and important part of creating a useful assessment battery. Critical to designing an assessment battery is knowing which instruments measure what skills (see Chapter 2).

According to Schneider and colleagues:

> Essentially, assessment is the scientific method applied on a small scale. The same procedures used to validate broad scientific theories are also applied to generate individualized case formulation of examinees. Ideally, you listen closely to your referrers and help them to articulate a clear set of referral questions that can be meaningfully answered by assessment. Then you generate a list of possible hypotheses from which you create a flexible assessment plan to evaluate those hypotheses. As new data and observations are gathered, you evaluate your hypotheses as you go. Often, hypotheses need to be revised or refined, prompting further rounds of planning, testing, and hypothesis evaluation until plausible explanations for the referral questions are found and you can update your case formulation.
>
> (Schneider et al. 2018: 129)

Possible Constellations

It is wise to think "what are the underpinnings and requirements of learning in each academic area?" When thinking about *reading*, the cluster of possibilities includes: phonemic awareness, knowledge of phonic rules including syllabication, morphology, automatic recognition of high-frequency words, and language skills including vocabulary, syntax, and grammar. Reading comprehension also requires adequate background knowledge.

In addition, comprehending *expository text* requires saliency determination (determining what is important in order to focus attention), subject-specific vocabulary, and knowledge of different text structures. Undergirding reading skills are hearing, auditory discrimination, vision acuity, binocular vision, visual

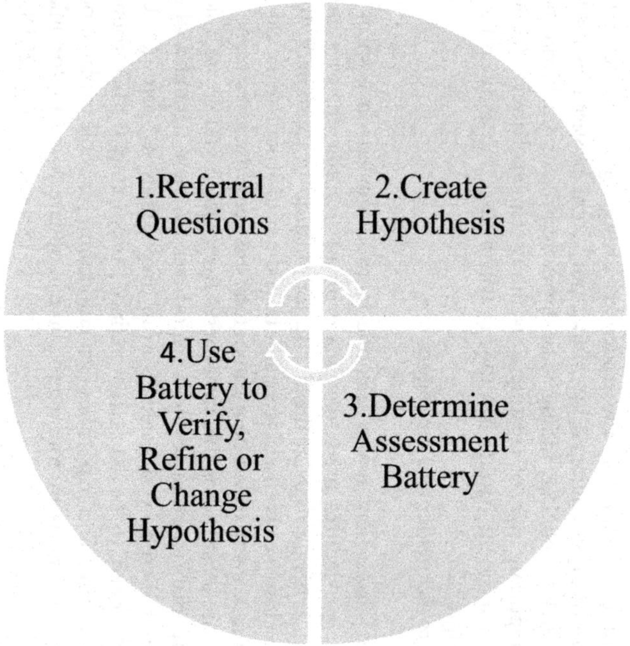

Figure 4.1 Hypothesis Testing

Creating the Student's Profile 67

perceptual skills (including visual memory and visual sequential memory), vocabulary, and language skills.

For *math* issues, consider strengths and weaknesses in number sense, understanding the patterns of number, calculation skills, automaticity with number facts, recalling math procedures, the ability to problem solve, and the specialized language of math. Math also requires strengths in sustained attention, working memory, adequate visual spatial skills, which includes visual sequential memory, attention to visual details and visual motor integration skills.

Written language is based on one's inner language. Therefore, the constellation for written language is: language (expressive and receptive), background knowledge, vocabulary, ideation (the ability to generate ideas), spelling, syntax, grammar, writing mechanics (punctuation and capitalization), orthographic knowledge and the recall for letter formation that support the development of handwriting skills. Written expression requires a synthesis of *all* of these skills, which is why it is so challenging for many students. This need for synthesis creates the highest demand for working memory as compared to other academic skills. The writer must create ideas, generate appropriate and varied vocabulary, sequence ideas while using proper capitalization, punctuation, and spelling. Writing also places a demand on visual motor integration skills. Written expression requires holding onto thoughts while writing. Remaining on topic requires focal maintenance and strong executive function skills. Editing through revisions can tax working memory.

By understanding the "constellations," one can develop an assessment plan that will test and refine a working hypothesis. Be prepared to add in other assessment measures, as new questions may occur. An example of this is when you first met Cassie and she brought you a drawing of a unicorn that she had made. It was detailed and had richly vibrant colors. You admired it and asked how long she took to draw it. She grabbed a nearby piece of paper and began sketching. You observed that she drew very quickly. So, what appeared to be an original drawing was likely an often practiced form. "Wow. You are drawing the unicorn so quickly," you said. Cassie nodded, "It's the only thing I draw. I draw it all the time!"

As she continued to draw you noted that her pencil grip changed from a typical dynamic tripod grasp to that of a static tripod grasp (where three fingers hold the pencil very near the pencil lead). This is a "less mature" grasp where the wrist and forearm are moving the pencil rather than her fingers. Does Cassie have difficulties with visual motor integration? You will watch her pencil skills when she performs the calculations on the Key Math-3. If she changes her grip frequently, shakes out her hand due to fatigue or cramping, or has any difficulties lining up the numerals, you will ask for permission to add in the Beery-Buktenica Developmental Test of Visual-Motor Integration, 6th edition (VMI-6).

Contributions of Non-Standardized Instruments

Many ETs use non-standardized measures. Some may be published and others are self-made. Both and have a history of good utility for the ET. I combine

68 *Creating the Student's Profile*

non-standardized measures (informal assessments) very often with standardized instruments. Non-standardized tools have many advantages. They can be created to gather the specific information needed. An informal tool can become "normed" because you are generally testing students from the same schools and/or community. ETs who create them become very attuned to what is a usual response to the items or tasks and what is an atypical response.

There are many benefits to using non-standardized assessments. The administration of informal instruments can be more fluid and readily adjusted without invalidating the results. One can readily change the order of the parts, add a question, remove questions, re-order the questions, skip some aspect and/or use simpler language. You may do all of that without invalidating the test scores because one is not required to follow the published "script" verbatim, prompts, and required protocols. Simply stated, these are not normed tests so you can do anything that seems clinically useful to gain insights into your working hypotheses.

In fact, less reliance on following all the correct administration procedures to produce valid test scores may allow the ET to *focus more* on the student's process and approach to each task. There will be more opportunities to interact, ask questions and probe while observing the student at work. You could insert some *diagnostic teaching* to see the effect:

- "What if you approach this problem by _____; would that help you?"
- "I see that you are a bit stuck. Try _____ and see if that works."
- "Do you remember what you did last time to get started?" If the student nods affirmatively, you might say, "Good. Try that again."
- "Would it help if there were fewer problems on the page? Okay, then I will cover up some."
- "Try using this book mark and see if that helps you to not skip lines when you read."
- "What if we were to take turns reading each paragraph? Let's see if that helps you remember more about what you just read."

Can you determine what each question is attempting to "test"?

However, sole reliance on informal or self-made measures may not create wholly accurate results. Suppose you are seeking certain information, so you create a tool and administer it. This could be a "closed loop" where one is essentially confirming your working hypothesis rather than considering other possibilities. If you do not administer other instruments, you may eliminate the opportunity to confirm or disprove your working hypothesis. Remember you may have created a tool to your own liking but whose *format* may impact the student's performance and influence the results.

Using Standards-Based, Criterion Reference Tests and Rubrics

When ETs use *standards-based* and/or *criterion reference* measures, they are attempting to answer questions more directly linked to intervention and remediation strategies. Generally, standards-based assessments are not normed but are designed to specifically align with state grade-level curricular standards and expectations. They may help to answer questions such as:

- Is the student working at grade-level?
- What parts of the curriculum has the student mastered?
- What specific aspects of the reading, math or language arts curriculum has the student not mastered?

For students attending independent schools, it can be clarifying to determine just how advanced the school curriculum's and expectations are compared to state standards. This can be especially illuminating when a family is considering a change in school for their child.

Criterion reference tests are sometimes termed "diagnostic tests" because they are designed to pinpoint the specific skills the student has already learned. One can quickly determine which discrete skills the student has mastered, and where the "gaps" are, which can be very useful. It is important to note that most formal assessments provide a limited number of items in each curricular area. Criterion reference tests have multiple items of each type allowing for more evidence when measuring specific skills. They are extremely helpful in formulating the client's learning goals and creating lessons for each session. Using these types of measures is how most ETs establish baseline data by which they measure a student's progress.

Rubrics can be very effective in evaluating student writing because they list standards and gradations in levels of quality. In a classroom setting, they are usually associated with a relatively complex or long-term assignment, such as a project, an essay, or a research paper (Andrade 2000). Just as students find writing may tax working memory, in my experience evaluating writing samples using a standardized assessment is the most difficult area to score. It also requires more time to learn how to give, administer to students and score than any other type of measure. Since most ETs do not need a standard score or percentile rank to work with a student in the area of written expression, having a well-crafted rubric is sufficient to evaluate a student's writing and begin remediation. Most schools have one you may ask for and adopt. The California Department of Education (2018) has an informative one available online for grades K–12, and other states have published them as well.

Link Hypothesis Testing with Observations and the Student's Spontaneous Remarks

During the assessment process, evidence starts to point to what might be occurring. After rapport has been built, an opportune time may come for the examiner to ask the student to respond to specific observations or ideas.

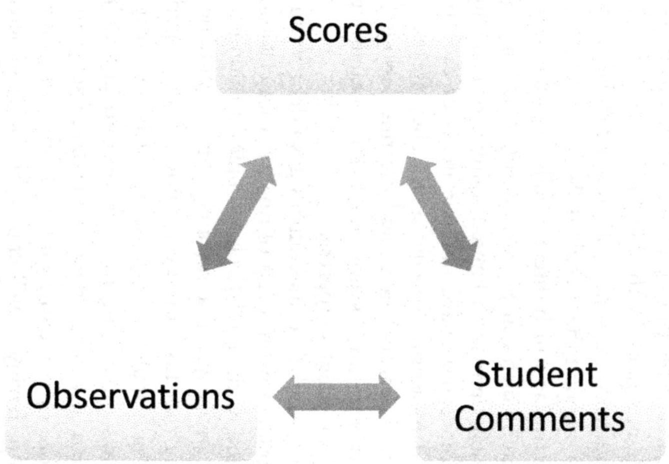

Scores

Student
Comments

Observations

Figure 4.2 Interaction Triangle

Creating the Student's Profile 71

Example 1: Colby

"Colby" is completing the first grade. His parents and teachers are worried about his reading skills. After he completed reading a very short passage from the Gray Oral Reading Test, Fifth Edition (GORT-5), composed of basic sight words and a few Consonant Vowel Consonant (CVC) words, I ask, "What are you doing to help yourself, Colby?" He answers, "I'm just looking at the words." Examiner: "It seems that you can recognize a lot of words (already measured in the Woodcock–Johnson IV Tests of Achievement Letter and Word Identification test), but when you see them in a story, it gets harder. Is that right?" I share my observations and hypothesis with the student seeking verification and encouraging further insights. (I always allow for the student's disagreement—which would be just as valuable.) Colby nods his agreement and adds a very helpful comment. "When I read stories, my eyes get tired and I skip lines. I usually read with a book marker to block off the lines under." Colby has just completed a vision examination, but the optometrist did not add in a binocular vision exam, which would have measured visual tracking and eye teaming, in addition to measuring visual acuity. Now there is an additional hypothesis to investigate. Is Colby experiencing binocular vision issues that could be affecting his acquisition of reading skills? Did you notice how Colby has verbalized a compensation strategy he uses to assist himself? In my experience, students can often be a valuable source of insight into their learning issues.

Example 2: Thomas

It is clear that, in the ninth grade, "Thomas" has difficulties comprehending grade-level expository texts. He reads with adequate accuracy and fluency and can generally grasp the main idea of a passage. However, when he does not have background knowledge or familiarity with the key vocabulary, his comprehension declines. In trying to answer a question on the GORT-5, Thomas stated, "I know I just read that … but I didn't really get it." The paucity of his knowledge of background information and lack of familiarity with content-specific vocabulary combine with his apparent difficulties with word retrieval based on your observations during the assessment. Reading complex science and social studies texts is very challenging. If one is qualified to administer some language assessments, the initial battery can be supplemented (with permission). Or, it can be recommended that Thomas be referred to a speech and language pathologist for a more in-depth look at his language skills.

Example 3: Anya

"Anya" is a sixth-grader who is struggling with reading. She is referred with questions about her reading skills and how to support her reading of expository texts. Her score on the Woodcock–Johnson IV Tests of Achievement

72   Creating the Student's Profile

(WJ-IV-ACH) Passage Comprehension test is a robust 63rd percentile rank for her age. Yet, on the Wechsler Individual Achievement Test, 3rd edition (WIAT-III) Reading Comprehension subtest, she scores at the 39th percentile rank for her age. Additionally, on the GORT-5, Anya scores at the 25th percentile rank for her age. These tests all have similar names. They all are testing reading comprehension, right? So why is there a marked difference in scores? These are all well-regarded tests. Which one is accurately measuring Anya's reading comprehension skill? One way to understand these differences in scores is to understand that each has differences in test construction and format. A reason for this is each test defines and measures reading comprehension differently.

The variance in constructs results in the dissimilarity of test format. A seasoned ET works to understand the underlying construct that is reflected in any test's format. These differences may significantly affect test scores. Interpretation of Anya's scores needs to be made with that understanding. So, what are the differences? On the WJ-IV-ACH a student reads silently. So, the ET cannot use it as a measure of reading accuracy or fluency. Word recognition, decoding skills, oral reading and reading fluency are measured discreetly in separate tests. Importantly, the WJ-IV-ACH uses a cloze procedure, where one must combine background knowledge, vocabulary, syntax, and grammar to select the single word that makes sense in the passage. The authors of the WJ-IV-ACH firmly believe that these *are* the essential skills that underlie reading comprehension. Therefore, that is what is being measured. Significantly, the reading "passages" are very brief. In class, Anya's teachers are expecting her to read long, sustained texts. Therefore, if Anya has good language and background knowledge, her Passage Comprehension score will be high, even though she may not be able to read the chapters assigned with good understanding. Scores on WJ-IV-ACH Passage Comprehension are often inflated compared to other reading comprehension measures since the passages are very brief and one can fill in the missing word if one's background knowledge, vocabulary, and sematic skills are strong.

On the WIAT III, a student reads grade-level passages. The passages are intended as "authentic measures" of actual classroom work, utilizing the different types of texts a student would encounter. Additionally, the student *may review* the passage while answering questions, which undermines checking for immediate recall and understanding. The grade-level passages use text passages slightly below, at, or slightly above grade level. Both factual and inferential questions are asked. One ends the assessment if the student has been successful at the grade level. If not, the ET applies the reverse rule going back to the previous grade level. So, Anya's differences in scores are the result of test format *and* the actual construct being measured. In fact, there is only a .79 correlation between the WJ-III-ACH Passage Comprehension and the WIAT-III Reading Comprehension subtest, which indicates they are not closely aligned (Shrank et al. 2001).

The GORT-5 measures reading comprehension using passages that increase in length and complexity. Many questions are open-ended and the subject cannot "look back" to aid recall. Reading accuracy and fluency are measured within the context of reading the passage. Anya's recall was not as good on the GORT-5. She answered factual questions better than open-ended ones. It would be very rare to use all three of these standardized measures with the same student. However, they are discussed here to compare the differences in test format. As an ET, one must use an understanding of test format to support or refine your working hypothesis. Always consider the language load, visual spatial processing, working memory demands, and visual motor requirements when thinking about variance between test or subtest scores. Use this understanding and combine it with information from other professional sources and from a variety of instruments to get a complete picture of student performance.

The Context of Assessment

The National Joint Committee on Learning Disabilities (1998) stresses that there is a need to examine the context as well as the purpose of assessment. The authors of the Essentials of Cross-Battery Assessment (Flanagan et al. 2013) name these other essential factors as the *ecology of assessment*. This refers to the factors in assessment that result from the assessment instrument itself (test format, construction, reliability, and validity), as well as the contributions from the student. Results may include the testing circumstances, mood of student, level of rapport established, and so on.

For example, some novice examiners only mark the incorrect responses. However, this practice highlights errors. Some students become very attuned to this and can become very sensitized; you may actually be skewing the results when only marking the errors. Mark every response. If one were to examine my protocol, one would notice a tremendous amount of writing in the margins of the record sheet. What else am I noting?

The Role of Observation

During assessment, strive to be a keen observer—not merely a recorder of correct and incorrect responses. I am marking student comments, my observations and questions that are occurring to me that will need to be investigated further. It is imperative to observe and note fluctuations in self-regulatory behaviors such as level of engagement, avoidance, pace, alertness, attention, sustained attention, mental energy, fatigue, effort, mental flexibility, and persistence. These are valuable clinical observations.

A student's response style may vary when different tasks are presented. Some of these differences may be explained by the interaction of the student and the test format. For example, consider the number of math problems on a page. How "crowded" does the page appear? Does the number of items

74 Creating the Student's Profile

and spatial arrangement on the page seem to visually overwhelm the student, or contribute to fatigue, or even an unwillingness to attempt a set of problems? When examining test construction and choosing test instruments, ask yourself these questions: What is the language load? How complex are the oral directions? How long is a verbal passage? Can the student have oral directions repeated? Are there visual cues to support material that is presented orally? Is the subtest timed? Does the student perform better when there is a time pressure (for some it aids in focus, though for most the time pressure adds cognitive load to the execution of a task)? Pair what you know (or suspect) about the individual's learning profile with what you have determined are the format or features of the subtest or test. Does a student do markedly different on one test than another when both purport to measure the same academic skill? Ponder this while thinking about the resulting score(s). Consider and closely examine each subtest's built-in cognitive demand and the student's response to each.

Become familiar enough with each test and its administration so that you are not focusing on *how* to administer the test. Be attentive to the student's response style, pace, body language, comments, and actions. Note examples of strategic planning, problem-solving, and use of language. Record the student's responses verbatim—not just whether responses are correct or incorrect. To do this, you will have to develop a "short-hand" for recording responses verbatim. These actions will enable the examiner to move beyond merely calculating a set of scores. While the derived scores are necessary, they are woefully incomplete in constructing a nuanced understanding of the learner's profile.

After completing a subtest or a battery, look for a pattern of strengths and weaknesses. Determine if this has helped to confirm your working hypothesis. Sometimes new questions have been generated. For example, no one mentioned language processing issues, but during assessment the student repeatedly asked for directions to be repeated. Now, a new question has emerged. What are the student's auditory memory and language processing skills?

On the second day, you notice that the student is not just asking for items and directions to be repeated, now he is staring solely at your mouth. Now, another question emerges. What is the known about the student's hearing? Has he had a recent audiological exam? Is there any history of a hearing loss or significant allergies that may impeded listening so he compensates by lip reading?

What if you notice that as the text grows more complex and the print is smaller and denser, another student begins to move much closer to the page or brings the reading material closer to her face or cocks her head to one side while reading. New questions emerge that need to be answered. What is known about the student's vision and acuity?

You noticed Cassie does not often use the sheet of paper provided for math problems even as the math problems grow more complex. Her formation of numerals is not consistent. Most are begun from the bottom. Often the numerals "stray" and are not lined up correctly in columns. You will definitely request permission to administer the Beery VMI-6. Do you see how careful

Creating the Student's Profile   75

observation can greatly contribute to hypothesis testing, case formulation and "ruling in," "ruling out" or adding to the initial referral questions?

Assessment is so much more than a set of derived scores. An effective assessment examines both quantitative and qualitative data. Assessment instruments, in and of themselves, are valuable tools but are usually incomplete answers to the referral questions. McGrew (in Shrank et al. 2001: 126) reminds us "the clinician is the instrument." Including your careful observations during the assessment process and the student's comments, all contribute to a more complete understanding of that student. No test can determine the best remediation plan nor can test results decide the work of each session. Those outcomes are the domain of a skilled educational therapist and some of the best reasons for conducting assessment.

Examining Assessment Results to Create the Student's Profile

In Chapter 3, you examined Cassie's math scores on the WJ-IV-ACH. Although her math skills are somewhat low, Cassie did not qualify for any special education services because she is "passing all her classes" and "no processing deficit was found." Having no processing deficit is excellent news. Then, why is Cassie struggling in math? Can you identity one clear possibility based on her scores on the WJ-IV-ACH? Later, you administered the Key Math-3, since it had not been given by the school district personnel, to delve more deeply into different math areas and to have the opportunity to watch her work. You heard Cassie mumbling, "Math is so stupid. Who cares about math, anyway?" Later, she remarked, "No calculator? That's ridiculous! How is anybody supposed to do this!" You noted that she did not use the paper supplied for calculations very often, and often "gave up" after sensing she could not readily solve a problem.

Study her scores on the WJ-IV-ACH and the Key Math-3. Think how the two tests' scores relate to each other or differ. Consider what you know about the construction of each test/subtest, its format, and the demands placed on the learner.

Cassie scored within the same range on the Applied Problems (WJ-IV-ACH) and Applications of the Key Math-3. Both measured her ability to use key elements in problems to determine the math operation and apply a math strategy or process needed to solve the problem. Her ability to perform basic calculations was also similar on Calculation (WJ-IV-ACH) and on Operations (Key Math-3). She did slightly better on the Operations Addition and Subtraction and Multiplication and Division subtest so let us examine each test's format. On the WJ-IV-ACH, the "boxes" where a student does the computation are 1.75 inches by 1.75 inches (about 3 square inches) per problem, whereas each computation space on the Key Math-3 is three inches by four inches (12 sq. inches) and the printed numbers are noticeably larger. Could that be a factor if Cassie has visual motor integration issues?

Table 4.1 Cassie's WJ-IV-ACH and Key Math-3 Scores

WJ-IV-ACH	Standard Score	Percentile Rank
Applied Problems	87	19
Calculations	86	15
Math Fact Fluency	78	7
Number Matrices	81	10
Key Math-3	**Subtest Composite Standard Score**	**Percentile Rank**
Basic Concepts	89	23
Operations	87	18
Applications	88	21

A careful item analysis of her work on these is necessary to fully appreciate what Cassie can and cannot do. Math Fact Fluency is measured *separately* on the WJ-IV-ACH. Here, her difficulty becomes very apparent. What effect might not knowing math facts automatically have on her other math skills? Lastly, Number Matrices (WJ-IV-ACH) requires a student to fill in the missing number from a grid. One must recognize number patterns and the relationship between numbers to do well on this test. There is no comparable subtest on the Key Math-3. Could Cassie's lack of math fact fluency be a factor here?

Look back at the Constellation suggested for math skills. Do you recognize some aspects of Cassie in it? David Geary (1994) was one of the first researchers who tried to connect "Mathematics Disorder" with neuropsychological deficits. He named three subtypes of deficits (echoed in Geary & Hoard 2005):

1   *Procedural* difficulties, where students present a delay in acquiring simple arithmetic strategies, which may be a result of verbal working memory deficits, but also deficits in conceptual knowledge.
2   *Semantic memory*, where students show deficits in retrieval of math facts because of a long-term memory deficit.
3   *Spatial* difficulties, in which students show deficits in the spatial representation of number.

Other researchers (Karagiannakis et al. 2014) have since added a *number knowledge* deficit. Most note that math learning disabilities are almost always multimodal (ibid.).

While Cassie may not have a math learning disability, she may have specific weaknesses in one or more areas. Can you identify it/them? If so, are you getting some ideas about how to support develop, and improve her math skills?

An Approach to Analyzing Assessment Scores

To assist in analyzing assessment scores, I make a list of the scores across instruments, comment and behaviors. I always create three lists, headed with a plus (+), minus (–) and a question mark (?). In the first (+) column, I make a list of strengths or "relative strengths." (Relative strengths are those which may not be average or above but they are the strongest area(s) for the student.) I begin by listing the strengths and relative strengths, positive working behaviors and spontaneous comments.

In the minus (–) list, I record the weaker scores or those that are "relatively weak." Relatively weak scores are those that may be in the average or above average range but are noticeably weaker than the areas of strength. Also included in this column are behaviors that demonstrate a lack of attention or persistence, and negative or self-deprecating comments.

The items in the question mark list (?) are those items that are puzzling (such as seeming contradictions between test scores) or other points would be

Table 4.2 Cassie's Strengths, Weaknesses, and Questions

+	−	?
Concerned parents	Math fact fluency (WJ-IV-ACH Math Fact Fluency 7th percentile rank)	Why the interest in robotics?
A mother who successfully advocated to have her assessed		What math facts does she know?
Commitment to working with an ET	Number patterns (WJ-IV-ACH Number Matrices 10th percentile rank)	Does she enjoy any area of math?
Verbal strengths (WISC-V)		Can you link her drumming with math?
Is passing all of her classes (IEP report)	Long division	Will you get to see the IEP teams' report, if so when?
Expresses her wishes and dislikes clearly	Multi-digit multiplication	
Enjoys reading (by report of her mother)	Fractions (common denominators, simplifying with greatest common factor)	Is a processing strength identified in the report?
Likes playing the drums (by report of her mother)		How/when does Cassie prepare for math tests?
No identified processing issue (IEP report)	Converting fractions into decimals and vice versa	Does she stay current on her math homework?
Relative strength in problem solving (19% Applied Problems WJ-IV & 21% Applications Key Math-3)	Limited use of paper when performing calculations (observation)	Can Cassie read music?
	Weak visual motor integration skills (Beery VMI 6th edition 9th percentile rank)	Does Cassie like playing games or solving puzzles?
Relative strength in performing math calculation in addition and subtraction—especially when there is extra space working space and the numbers are larger (Key Math-3 Written Computation Examinee Booklet (Operations))	Inefficient writing of numerals (observation)	Does she like to cook or bake?
	Reliance on calculator (observation)	Has she had a recent vision exam?
	Cassie: "One-third is bigger than one-fourth? How is that even possible? Four is bigger than three!"	

Creating the Student's Profile 79

helpful to know. Table 4.2 shows an example of a completed list of strengths, weaknesses, and questions.

This approach may help you determine the findings, prepare to present orally (see Chapter 6), and write a strengths-based report that utilizes Cassie's abiding interests in some of the recommendations (see Chapter 5).

Self-review questions for students and professionals

1 What techniques do you use to create a shared perception of a student's struggles?
2 Do you understand the term "constellations" as used in this chapter?
3 How do you form a working hypothesis?
4 What are the advantages of using non-standardized instruments?
5 What are some of your favorite informal instruments? Why do you value them?
6 How do you decide when to use them?
7 What are some of disadvantages of using non-standardized instruments?
8 Does Cassie's math profile relate to any of the math "constellations"? If so, which one(s)?
9 Since Cassie is in the beginning of the 6th grade, how much of a factor is her lack of math fact automaticity?
10 What effect might weak visual motor integration skills have on math acquisition?
11 At this point, can you summarize the key findings for Cassie?

Resources

Beery-Buktenica Developmental Test of Visual-Motor Integration: www.pearsona ssessments.com
Common Core Standards for Mathematical Content: www.corestandards.org/Math/ Practice/
Fuchs, L. S. & Fuchs, D. (2002). Mathematical Problem-Solving Profiles of Students with Mathematics Disabilities with and Without Comorbid Reading Disabilities. *Journal of Learning Disabilities*, 35: 557–563.
Fuchs, L. S. & Fuchs, D. (2005). Enhancing Mathematical Problem-Solving for Students with Disabilities. *Journal of Special Education*, 39: 45–57.
Gray Oral Reading Test 5th Edition (GORT-5): www.proedinc.com
Key Math-3 Diagnostic Assessment: www.pearsonassessments.com
Lindamood, P. C. & Lindamood, P. (2003). *Lindamood Auditory Conceptualization Test (LAC-3)*. Austin, TX: Pearson Education.
Marshall, M. & Matthaei, D. (2013). Guidelines for Conducting Standardized Assessment. The Educational Therapist, 34(1): 26–28.
Mather, N. & Wendling, B. (2003). Instructional Implications from the Woodcock-Johnson III. In F. A. Schrank & D. F. Flanagan (Eds.), *WJ III Clinical Use and Interpretation: Scientist Practitioner Perspectives* (pp. 93–124). New York: Academic Press.

80 Creating the Student's Profile

Neukrug, E. S. & Fawcett, R. C. (2009). *Essentials of Testing and Assessment: A Practical Guide for Counselors, Social Workers, and Psychologists* (2nd ed.). Pacific Grove, CA: Brooks/Cole Publishing Co.

Shrank, F. & Flanagan, D. P. (Ed.). (2003). *Clinical Use and Interpretation of the WJ III.* Burlington, MA: Elsevier.

WIAT-III. (2009). *Wechsler Individual Achievement Test, 3rd Edition (WIAT-III).* New York: Pearson.

Wiederholt, J. L. & Bryant, B. R. (2012) *Gray Oral Reading Test, Fifth Edition (GORT-5).* Austin, TX: Pearson Education.

References

Andrade, H. G. (2000). Using Rubrics to Promote Thinking and Learning. *ASCD,* 57(5).

California Department of Education. (2018). English Language Proficiency Assessments for California Writing Rubrics for the English Language Proficiency Assessments for California. Retrieved from www.elpac.org/s/pdf/ELPAC_Writing-Rubrics.pdf

Flanagan, D. P., Ortiz, S. O. & Alfonso, V. C. (2013). *Essentials of Cross-Battery Assessment,* 3rd edition. New York: Wiley.

Geary, D. C. (1994). *Children's Mathematical Development: Research and Practical Applications.* Washington, DC: American Psychological Association.

Geary, D. C. & Hoard, M. (2005). Learning Disabilities in Arithmetic and Mathematics: Theoretical and Empirical Perspectives. In J. I. D. Campbell (Ed.), *Handbook of Mathematical Cognition,* 253–267. New York: Psychology Press.

Karagiannakis, G., Baccaglini-Frank, A., Papadatos, Y. (2014) Mathematical Learning Difficulties Subtypes Classifications. *Frontiers in Human Neuroscience,* 8: 57.

National Joint Committee on Learning Disabilities. (1998). Operationalizing the NJCLD Definition of Learning Disabilities for Ongoing Assessment in Schools. *ASHA,* 40 (Suppl. 18).

Schneider, J. W., Lichtenberger, E. O., Mather, N., Kaufman, N. & Kaufman, N. (2018). *Essentials of Assessment Report Writing,* 2nd edition. Hoboken, NJ: John Wiley & Sons.

Shrank, F., McGrew, K. & Woodcock, R. W. (2001). *Woodcock-Johnson III Tests of Achievement. Assessment Service Bulletin.* New York: Pearson Publishing.

5 Writing a High-Quality Assessment Report

"We waited so long to receive a written copy of this report, and frankly, I don't understand it or understand how it will help our daughter!" We have all read extensive reports written by allied professionals such as educational psychologists and neuropsychologists that were very costly, are over twenty pages long, and not readily understandable. In fact, as an ET, I have been paid in my private practice to "translate" these reports for parents or to "distill" these reports into something useful for school personnel when employed by an independent school.

Introduction

How does an educational therapist write a report that is clear, concise, professional in tone relevant, and useful? There are many crucial elements:

- establishing a clear purpose for the report;
- knowing the audience;
- determining the findings;
- avoiding jargon;
- focusing on the individual and not the scores;
- writing a strengths-based report;
- synthesizing information in an organized and analytic manner;
- using a professional voice; and
- creating individualized recommendations.

This chapter will guide you through crafting each critical element to write a cogent document.

Establish a Purpose

Like any piece of good writing, an assessment report is written with a clear sense of purpose. The purposes for an educational therapy report are to describe the client and the educational questions being asked, provide the results of the assessments administered, explain their relevance to the referring

82 *Writing a High-Quality Assessment Report*

questions, and present recommendations for the future. The report generally starts with a background section describing the individual, including age, grade, relevant educational history, findings from other professionals and then states the questions that brought the individual and his family to the ET. Questions might be, "Why is my second grader struggling to learn to read?" or "Why does my 7th-grader find math so very difficult?" or "Why can't my highly verbal 5th-grader write well?"

Know the Audience

An experienced writer always considers the intended audience for the report. The primary audience for an assessment report is usually the student and her/his family so endeavor to write clearly and simply. Describe what the student can and cannot do. For an ET in private practice, the client and her family are the ones who pay for the assessment; parents should be able to read the document and have it made sense to them. Be clear of the intended audience and your purpose. Because ETs generally do not assess cognitive skills and therefore do not "determine eligibility," especially in terms of the discrepancy model, assessment serves a vastly different purpose. David Roth, then the Director of Special Education in Piedmont Unified School District, wrote in *The Educational Therapist* about the tensions these differences can create:

> Public school assessments are conducted for the purpose of determining whether the student meets the criteria for receiving services in accordance with regulations. Private assessments are conducted for the purpose of diagnosing the underlying reasons for school problems or learning disorders. A private practitioner may diagnose a student with a learning disorder; however, if the student has a history of meeting grade appropriate standards in the classroom, the student does not necessarily qualify for special education services provided by the school district.
>
> (Roth 2005: 5)

Actually, ETs do not diagnose unless they have additional and specific training and licensure that enables them to do so. Any ET who represents themselves as providing a diagnosis as their purpose may be misleading the parent(s) and acting contrary to the code of ethics (see Chapter 2).

Well-intended ETs can feel thwarted when they share their assessment results with a school district. They have prepared a very thoughtful and nuanced description of why the student is struggling. The ET finds the evidence compelling and seeks the district's acknowledgement of that struggle and provision of services (or at least accommodations) for the student. However, the district is answering a different question: Is the student eligible for services under special education law? Or, is the student still eligible for services? The district's question is not whether the student is struggling and/or becoming overwhelmed in attempting to meet standards or "keep up" with

Writing a High-Quality Assessment Report 83

grade-level expectations, but is the child *making adequate progress?* Perhaps, the ET is more aware of the emotional toll of "keeping up." I have the image of a shorebird that appears to be floating effortlessly across the top of the water. However, if one were able to see *under* the water, the bird's legs would be paddling furiously to keep up with the flow and demands of the current.

Not understanding the differences between the ET's and district's motivations for assessment, one's report at an IEP meeting may be turned aside and any crucial findings jeopardized and/or dismissed. This does not benefit the student, the parents, the IEP process, nor demonstrate what a well-trained ET *can* do.

Determine the Findings

I use the term *findings* to record and discuss the significant results. Scores, task analysis, discussion of error patterns and observations support each finding. Student comments that are especially illustrative are included. Findings can be strengths or weakness but they are the *key points* in understanding the student's current learning profile and in developing a cogent treatment plan. Each finding should be included in the final summary and lead directly to goals, recommendations, and interventions. They may provide suggestions for changes in classroom instruction and for appropriate classroom accommodations.

To ensure that I do not forget to link a finding to a treatment goal, I place a notation in the recommendations as I am writing the body of the report. Example: *Finding: Jeremy has a well-developed oral vocabulary but his written work uses short sentences and simple words.* My placeholder note in recommendations would be "Increase sentence complexity; improve and vary vocabulary in written work."

At this point, consider Cassie's math skills. In Chapter 4, did you determine the key findings? If not, refer back to the questions posed in the self-review questions for students and professionals.

Key Findings for Cassie—A Narrative

In my view, Cassie is on the edge of a very dangerous precipice. These findings will be shared with her parents, her 6th-grade math teacher, and Cassie herself (see the Conclusion in Chapter 6), although the language may be altered a bit, depending on the audience. However, all of these findings are important and valid. Cassie may not have a diagnosed math disability, but her math skills are significantly below grade level, primarily hampered by her lack of math fact automaticity and reliance on a calculator—both of which have affected her understanding of number patterns. She recalls addition and subtraction facts more readily than multiplication and division. Cassie currently is quite reliant on using her calculator, but that is understandable given her limitations with math facts. She commits little work to paper, but that may be because she has reasonably strong working memory and processing skills, as identified by the

84 Writing a High-Quality Assessment Report

WISC-V and due to the recently identified visual motor integration issue (Beery VMI 9th percentile rank for her age). In the ensuing years, math problems will become increasing complex, requiring multi-stepped problem solving. She will need to keep track of her calculations to be successful. In addition, most math teachers in middle school and high school require students "to show their work." Improving her visual motor skills for writing numerals efficiently and lining up columns of numbers correctly are essential skills to be mastered this year.

It is important to recognize that Cassie's math skills are closer to the 3rd-grade level, according to the national Common Core Math Standards which are "a balanced combination of procedure and understanding" (www.coresta ndards.org/Math). She has a strength in Standard 1: "Mathematically proficient students start by explaining to themselves the meaning of a problem and looking for entry points to its solution." Cassie was reliably able to decide which math procedure to use to solve a problem, even when she did not have the calculations skills to solve it correctly. She is weak in Standard 7, which expresses that "Mathematically proficient students look closely to discern a pattern or structure." Cassie is not clear about number patterns and the relationship between numbers, which are skills that need to be developed. Finally, she is notably weak in Standard 4, "Mathematically proficient students can apply the mathematics they know to solve problems arising in everyday life, society, and the workplace." Remember that Cassie said she did not know why anyone cared about math. She has yet to connect math with daily practical life skills.

Avoid Professional Jargon

If it is necessary to use a specific professional term, describe it clearly. But the ET also needs to consider the secondary audience which includes teachers and other educational professionals who may also read the report. A high-quality assessment report needs to be understood by multiple audiences. A professional can always read a report written for the parent and teacher. The converse is not true—the parent and teacher may not understand a report that is written primarily for an allied professional.

Focus on the Individual, not the Scores

A high-quality assessment report should resonate deeply with parents. They should say, "Yes, that's my kid." They should experience "ah ha!" moments of new insights about their child. "Now I understand why my child is having so much difficulty with ..." Focus on the student being evaluated and not on the scores. Task analysis, error analysis and knowledge of each test's construction can assist in developing a detailed summary about the student's strengths and weaknesses that the parents can see. Cassie's parents remarked, "We see now that her math skills aren't so terrible. She needs to finally learn those pesky

Writing a High-Quality Assessment Report 85

math facts! It's good to know her math calculation skills and problem solving are pretty good. But, we need to do something about her attitude."

A well-written report answers the referral questions using test scores *and* qualitative information. An informative report summarizes, synthesizes and adds in student comment while interpreting the qualitative and quantitative data:

> Because testing data are gathered during an assessment, some evaluators spend too much time writing about the test scores rather than about what those scores mean. ... Because the sheer amount of data can be over-whelming, it seems easier to describe the test and obtained scores ... Unfortunately, when scores become the focal point of the report, the person being assessed seems to disappear in the array of numbers.
>
> (Lichtenberger et al. 2004: 5)

The focus of your report should be on what the scores mean. A well-synthe-sized and well-summarized report of findings will aid in developing compelling recommendations, interventions and treatment plans.

Professionals who have trained in assessment in public schools typically write only a part of what becomes the final report contained in the Individualized Education Plan (IEP). Assessors in public schools are usually cautioned against going beyond reporting the scores because eligibility and re-qualifying for ser-vices are partially based on standard test scores produced by different assessors (Resource Specialist, Speech and Language Therapist, School Psychologist and others). The language style of someone writing as a part of a school team is less precise. It often has a softened or "waffling" tone. "It *may be* that Samuel is struggling with math concepts" or "Lina *seems to be having* some difficulty with writing in complete sentences." Writing as an individual assessor is quite dif-ferent. An ET continues assessing until a definitive statement can be made. Here are some examples:

- Samuel demonstrated well-developed calculation skills as evidenced by his performance on the WJ IV ACH "Calculation" test where he performed at the 73rd percentile; however, he struggles with determining number patterns "Number Matrices" (17th percentile).
- Lina has well-developed oral vocabulary skills (88th percentile), according to her score on the Peabody Picture Vocabulary 5th Edition. Yet, her subtest scores on the Test of Written Language 4th Edition Contextual Vocabulary (24th percentile) show that she is not able to utilize her strong oral vocabulary when writing.

Remember that the *intent* is to clearly describe what the student *can* and cannot do. Novice report writers often become bogged down describing each test and in explaining the scores. Experienced writers also convey *what the scores mean*. A seasoned professional is technically accurate without being overly simplistic.

86 *Writing a High-Quality Assessment Report*

One should not allow the individual to become lost in a sea of standard scores and percentiles. Remain focused on the individual client or student.

Sometimes a new issue becomes apparent while conducting the assessment. Think of Camille in Chapter 1 and how she was concerned about her math skills. Recall that you observed Cassie's difficulties with visual motor integration and forming numbers efficiently. If you are going to administer additional standardized tests, obtain written permission to administer them, assuming your skills and training allow you to use them. If additional assessment is outside your purview, a referral to an *allied professional* should become one of the recommendations.

Write a Strengths-based Report

In the past, most reports focused on an individual's deficits. This practice likely developed because a student qualified for special education services by quantifying their deficits. "In a typical IEP meeting, not much time is given to looking at a child's strengths. Strengths are covered at the beginning of the meeting, and the rest of the time is focused on deficits" (Rawe undated).

Rather than merely providing a cursory comment or two, a strengths-based report is designed to highlight the assets and abilities that can be harnessed and leveraged to address areas of weakness. A strengths-based approach is a shift away from the "what's wrong" question and provides, instead, a more useful holistic 360-degree view of the student. In the case of Cassie, much is now known about her math skills and interests. Cassie's parents commented excitedly, "Cassie wants to learn how to build things? We didn't know that! That's wonderful! We can see if she is interested in carpentry or building sets since the middle school has a great drama program. Those use math!"

Helping the student to recognize strengths, preferences and affinities (deep and abiding interests) increases the possibilities for greater self-awareness which may lead to developing greater self-advocacy. This approach can assist teachers in seeing the student in a more positive light, which may initiate more empathy and motivate the teacher(s) to try new approaches in the classroom. Similarly, parents may re-visit their overly pessimistic view the of their student and the current situation. This approach encourages customization of the intervention approaches and recommendations. Incorporating more strengths-based findings encourages the team to consider the student in the school, home and community environments and creates language which takes a longer and more positive view forward.

Synthesize Information in a Clear, Organized, and Analytical Manner

In preparing to write an assessment report, I make the "+/−/?" list of scores, comments and behaviors as illustrated in Chapter 4. The items in the question

Writing a High-Quality Assessment Report 87

mark list (?) are those things that are puzzling and need further consideration or might need to be answered by a referral to an allied professional.

For example, before I can write a report, I try to answer the questions in the question mark column, like this:

Why the interest in robotics?	She wants to build things
Will the robotics club accommodate a student whose math skills are not strong?	No, they will not
What math facts does she know?	Yes
Does she enjoy any area of math?	Not yet
Can you link her drumming with math?	Not certain
Will you get to see the IEP teams report, if so when?	Yes
Is a processing strength identified in the report?	Yes
How/when does Cassie prepare for math tests?	Talk to Cassie during sessions
Does she stay current on her math homework?	Talk to Cassie during sessions
Can Cassie read music?	No
Does Cassie play any games or like solving puzzles?	Yes, verbal logic puzzles
Does she like to cook or bake?	Yes, is beginning to cook
Has she had a recent vision exam?	Yes, results unremarkable

Interestingly, I just had a conversation with a former student who is a very experienced ET. She volunteered that she is still using the "+/–/?" method while reading the reports from allied professionals, including neuropsychologists. Reading others' reports using this method is something I have not utilized! In order to write a well-written report, one must come to see the assessment results as a pattern of verified strengths and weaknesses. If you do not have a method you use consistently, try using the "+/–/?" method to help you identify the patterns.

In Cassie's case, the school psychologist's report was received and identified her verbal strengths. This would be summarized in the Background Section of the written report. I know which math facts she knows and which ones she does not. That information would be included the findings section of the report. I learned that Cassie cannot read music and why she is interested in the robotics club. These will assist in personalizing the Recommendations in the report. There are still some school-based questions to be answered in a conversation with Cassie or her math teacher. It is essential that school-based recommendations suit the school's philosophy and are respectful of the teacher's class policies and time. For Cassie, there is no current need to refer on to other allied professionals since she was recently assessed by the IEP team and that evaluation included a cognitive assessment.

88 *Writing a High-Quality Assessment Report*

Your assessment document should integrate and synthesize complex information and present the results in an organized way. The ET uses headings and subheadings with adequate spaces between them so that the format is inviting, instead of daunting, to the reader. ETs frequently give the results (test scores) of all assessment measures in an appendix at the end of the document. The body of the report should focus on the most relevant findings and does not need to describe each and every test given. The narrative describes the measures, compares and contrasts them, and explains their meaning. The report needs to be concise rather than verbose. Many seek to write a report that is no more than ten pages in length, not including the appendix listing the scores. A well-written shorter report usually has greater impact than a rambling 24-page one. The ET is careful to include learning strengths as well as weaknesses and then goes on to make recommendations of appropriate interventions and/or accommodations. The individual and her family want to understand *why* certain problems exist and to have a *detailed plan* presented to address the difficulties while acknowledging his strengths.

Remember the Reasons for Conducting an Assessment

Answering those initial questions is essential to writing an effective assessment report. It is very helpful to have laid out the scores across tests and subtests to look for patterns. Determining a pattern of strengths and weaknesses will help you decide what are the key findings. These are the aspects to highlight in your report. To write clearly, you must know what you wish to convey. Interestingly, some may use a draft of a written report to help them understand the findings. For those, synthesis occurs *in the writing process*. If you are one of these ETs, recognize that you are writing a first draft because it helps you clarify your understanding. It is not the final report itself. That will come later, so give yourself adequate time to write and revise.

Write in a Professional Voice

Another goal is to clearly communicate your findings. In general, simple words and concise sentences often create meaning. One factor that contributes to good writing is ensuring that the text has unity. Good writers often accomplish unity through the use of cohesion (using words that help connect ideas and clarify the relationships among ideas). "Cohesive ties help achieve continuity in writing by linking ideas across time, by cause and-effect, by admission, or by contrast" (Bates 2000, quoted in Lichtenberger et al. 2004: 96). "A common error in reports is that the writer assumes that the indentation of a paragraph signals a transition. Regardless of indentation, an abrupt shift in topic makes writing seem disjointed" (Lichtenberger et al. 2004: 12). I have found a way to write more clearly, as you can see below.

Writing a High-Quality Assessment Report 89

Writing with Bullet Points

It is very challenging to create a cohesive narrative report that responds to all the conventions of formal writing. When I read graduate students' assessment reports, the verb tenses are often inconsistent. It was a revelation to read a very expensive and extensive twenty-four-page report written by a neuropsychologist that utilized headings and bullet points. The flow was much better than other lengthy reports I had read. The shifts between topic were more accessible. The data points and examples stood out more clearly. All in all, it was easier to understand. When asked, the parents stated it was fairly comprehensible and the reasons for the recommendations seemed logical. At that moment (several years ago), I adopted the headings and bullet point format. I still write many sections in the usual narrative fashion. The *reason for referral, background information, summary of previous evaluations* and final *summary* are all written in a narrative following the appropriate heading. However, the *assessment findings*, including spontaneous student comments, and my observations of student behaviors while conducting the assessment are all listed in a bulleted format under the appropriate heading (Example: Reading Skills, Visual Perceptual Skills, Math Skills, Written Language, Visual Motor Integration and Fine Motor Skills or whatever domains were accessed). By grouping the related assessment results, observations, and student comments, cohesiveness is *greatly* enhanced. The key findings stand out.

Sections in a Written Report

A well-written report follows some conventions. Nearly every assessment report written by an educational psychologist or ET utilizes a similar format. It can be helpful to use the format's outline to organize the pertinent information. Include, in this order:

1 Identifying information: include the student's name; date of birth, student's age and grade; tests used; assessor's name and title; dates of evaluation; name of school; parents' names and teachers' names.
2 Reason for referral: identify the person who referred the student; discuss the reason for referral; identify the specific concerns and the purpose for the evaluation.
3 Background information: include relevant family history and current family constellations, relevant developmental and medical history; review and briefly summarize educational history, including changes in schools, retention, services provided.
4 School observations (if conducted).
5 Previous evaluations: summarize those results.
6 Tests administered: list the tests administered. List persons Interviewed, such as teachers (if done).

90 *Writing a High-Quality Assessment Report*

7 Behavioral observation: observations made during assessment; these may be incorporated into the narrative of test findings.

8 Assessment findings: I use the term *findings* to indicate what are the key points to emphasize. They are the "take away" for the parents and teachers and are a distillation of important data points or conclusions. I report scores in bulleted section of the report. One may list the actual scores in this section or attach them in an appendix. Integrate and interpret data from all of the contributing and supporting data such as work samples and a student's spontaneous comments.

9 Summary: briefly restate test results and state the implications of these results or conclusions drawn. Do not include new information in this section. This summary should lead the reader(s) to your specific recommendations and underscore *why* each is made.

10 Recommendations: list appropriate interventions, methodologies or strategies. Provide practical interventions based on the specific student's strengths and weaknesses. It is best to state who is responsible. Accommodations can be suggested here. For a more detailed list of what to include in each section see Mather and Jaffe (2016). This is also an excellent resource for viewing many written reports. To see exemplary models of how to write each section, read *Essentials of Assessment Report Writing*, 2nd edition (Schneider et al. 2018).

The Nature of Recommendations

The focus of the recommendations is on the specific person evaluated. Recommendations are developed for the individual, are guided by the specific referral questions, and should follow directly from the summarized findings. Formulate each recommendation with thoughtfulness and care. Be realistic but respectful. Avoid using words like "must" and "should." You may suggest specific programs or methodologies as examples but do not be *overly prescriptive*. Example: To improve John's reading fluency, programs such as Read Naturally, Great Leaps or One Minute Readers are recommended. Do *not* write: "John needs to use One Minute Readers." Recommendations should not be generic. Recommendations that do not seem personalized or individualized may be ignored. It can be helpful to separate out recommendations using headings such as: *Home, School*, the *Student* and *Outside Support*. This helps to signal who is responsible for taking these actions. Note any further testing or referrals to allied professionals and the rationale for recommending additional testing or referral.

SMART Goals and Strength-based Recommendations

Public school special educators are required to write a broad goal statement that includes a specific goal and measurable outcome. See this example from Rawe (undated): "Given fourth-grade level (4.0) reading material, Nura will

Writing a High-Quality Assessment Report 91

write three details from the passage in her own words with 85% accuracy on three out of four consecutive assignments." The article encouraging using strength-based goals re-wrote the above goal to be this:

> Given fourth-grade level (4.0) reading material on nonfiction topics, Nura *will deploy her love of learning and her interest in science and history* to write three details from the passage in her own words with 85% accuracy on three out of four consecutive assignments.

> (Rawe undated)

ETs write specific recommendations. Keep the recommendations achievable and measurable. SMART is an acronym borrowed from business or project management for setting goals that are **S**pecific, **M**easurable, **A**chievable, **R**elevant (or **R**ealistic) and **T**ime-based. As you write recommendations consider these factors. Make certain your recommendations are tailored to each student. Many assessments that are scored by a computer program can create goal statements that are "written and reviewed by experts in the field of special education" (Lichtenberger & Breaux 2010: 35). And the goal statements "include recommended intervention tasks and activities … with multiple choice options and spaces to fill in the blank to assist examiners in writing goals that are specific, measurable, and customizable for a student's individualized educational plan" (ibid.: 35). While this "short cut" may be appealing, I exhort others to do their own analysis and create truly individualized recommendations. It may be permissible to use the computer-generated "interventions" after you have drafted your recommendations as a way to verify you have thought through all of the possibilities.

List recommendations in order of priority. Suggest a time frame for interventions. Example: This team can meet back in three months to gauge progress and develop new goals, if needed. Do not overwhelm the reader with too many recommendations. They should be direct and positive. The best ones are strength-based. "Given Michael's difficulty with organizing …" and "In view of Margo's difficulty with …" are not strengths-based recommendations as both focus only on areas of deficits. Look back at Table 4.2, which lists Cassie's strengths, weaknesses and questions. Do you see how answering the questions is essential to writing some strengths-based recommendations?

In addition, I always try to include and represent the student's perceptions of their own experience as a learner. I add into my assessment battery a simple question directed at deriving the student's experience in school: "If you could change one thing about school, what would it be?" (For an adult client the question could be, "If you could change one thing at work, what would it be?") Often, the answer is surprisingly poignant and can be made a part of a school-based meeting. For example, Cassie sighed, "I do enough math at school. No math homework, please." This wish will need to be discussed with the math teacher to determine what might be possible before anything is written in a report (see Chapter 6).

92 *Writing a High-Quality Assessment Report*

For Cassie, the recommendations might look like those below though the list is quite inclusive and would likely be for a whole year. It is imperative to have conversations with others and get agreement before you "assign" a responsibility. In the examples below, I have inserted some rationales for the recommendation (because I want the reader to understand my thinking process, although I would not include this in an actual written report).

Home and Student

- Cassie will do hand strengthening and finger identification movement exercises as a "warm up" before doing any written homework. Rationale: These are not difficult or onerous exercises and emphasizes that like an athlete stretches *before* running, paying attention to building up the hand muscles will be helpful.
- She will use pencil and paper dot-to-dot exercises and mazes (supplied by her ET) to increase visual motor integration skills. Cassie will commit to doing 5 exercises per week.
- She will use binder paper turned so that the lines run vertically to do math homework as an assist in keeping numbers correctly lined up.
- Cassie will do 10 minutes of math fact practice 5 days per week using the math fact three-corner cards (see Resources). Rationale: These cards teach the relationship of numbers which "regular" math fact flash cards cannot due and reinforce the inverse nature of multiplication and division (and/or addition and subtraction).
- Her math teacher has agreed that her math homework time will be reduced by 10 minutes for doing her daily math fact practice and her math homework will not exceed 30 minutes per weekday.
- Cassie might enjoy drumming to the math facts (5 drum beat × 6 drum beat = drum roll 30).
- Cassie's parents suggested she might take drumming lessons as soon as she learns all her math facts, if she would like them.
- Cassie will calculate her allowance and expenditures regularly. And/or she can look at the supermarket adds to calculate the cost of ingredients for a dish she is cooking or compute the sale prices on a set of ingredients to evaluate the discount.
- Ask Cassie if she would like to join the set-building crew in the school's afterschool drama program. Rationale: Cassie wants to "build things."
- Cassie and her parents can find a carpentry class often offered in the area during the summer months. Rationale: Cassie wants to "build things."

School

- Cassie's math teacher agrees to scheduling a bi-weekly conversation with the ET to coordinate and facilitate approaches and responses to Cassie's ongoing instruction and math needs.

He has agreed that Cassie will be required to work for no more than 30 minutes daily on her math homework. Rationale: This responds (somewhat) to Cassie's wish for no math homework.

- In acknowledgement that Cassie is doing math on the days she is working with her ET, no more than 5 problems will be assigned as homework on those days.
- Her math teacher has agreed to institute a new policy that the entire class will be required to do first half of the assigned classwork without the use a calculator.

Outside Support with the Educational Therapist

- The ET will have regular communication with Cassie's math teacher to coordinate and facilitate approaches and responses to Cassie's ongoing instruction in class.
- The ET will provide pencil and paper dot-to dots exercises and mazes to increase Cassie's visual motor integration skills. (If adequate progress is not evident in 6 weeks, consider a referral to an occupational therapist.)
- Cassie needs to master her basic math facts in the four whole number operations. She should know here addition, subtraction facts to 20 (e.g., 9 + 8 = 17) and her multiplication and division facts to 12 (12 × 12 = 144). This should have the effect of improving her fraction and decimal skills, as well.
- Cassie will chart her progress in mastering the times table each week during a session. Rationale: There is research demonstrating that when a student charts her/his progress, there is more engagement and more rapid skill acquisition (Fuchs & Fuchs 2002; Mazzocco 2008; McDougall et al. 1998, 2006).
- Cassie should work on looking for patterns in the addition and multiplication tables. This will increase her speed and awareness of number patterns. She should also work on seeing the inverse relationships of addition and subtraction, multiplication and division. (e.g., 3 + 9 = 12, so 9 = 12 − 3; and 9 times 6 = 54, so 54 ÷ 9 = 6). Use of the three-corner cards is recommended.
- Cassie should review place value as it applies to whole numbers and the carry over to the decimal system (hundreds, tens, ones, tenths, hundredths, etc.).
- Cassie should practice multi-digit multiplication and division to be sure her algorithms are correct and automatic. She can record them in her "Memory Book" for reference. Rationale: This supports Cassie's verbal skills in her "Memory Book" she will record, in her own words, the algorithm and step-by-step process of solving different types of problems. Each is accompanied by her illustration of each step (see Resources).
- Cassie should improve her number sense and estimation skills by playing online games such as those in Motion Math (see Resources).

94 Writing a High-Quality Assessment Report

- Cassie can create different types of real world "word problems" and ask her ET to solve them. (Cassie must determine the operation(s) needed and be able to solve each before she can "assign" them to her ET.) Rationale: Cassie has verbal strengths which she can use to support her "real world" understanding and application of math.
- By the end of 6th grade, Cassie needs to learn the math theory concepts of factors, multiples, and prime numbers for use with fractions and pre-algebra skills.
- Cassie needs to develop a good understanding of the relationships between fractions, decimals, and percentages, and how each represents parts of a whole. She should learn to convert from one type to the others (e.g., ¼ = 0.25 = 25%) It is suggested Cassie do art activities such as *Using Art to Teach Fractions Decimal and Percent Equivalents* (see Resources) which colorfully illustrate these relationships. Rationale: I am thinking of Cassie's colorful unicorn drawing.

In sum, the recommendations are a "road map" for the future. Keep them individualized, thoughtful, organized, and achievable. ETs should be wary of using computer-generated recommendations. When I read them in others' reports, they seem generic, impersonal, and disingenuous.

Report Writing Dos

- Use proper grammar, punctuation and spelling in the report.
- Use the past tense in describing the subject's history.
- Use the past tense in describing the subject's behaviors during assessment.
- Use past tense to describe test results. (Your assessment took place prior to the writing of the report and your oral presentation.)
- Use present tense to describe current circumstance such as grade level or occupation.
- Write from an outline or from a list of key findings with related evidence (scores, observations, student comments, or behaviors)
- Create a personal "thesaurus" to vary frequently used phrases. (How many different ways can you say "has difficulty with"?)
- Connect related points with well-crafted sentences. Consider using "bullet points" for the findings.
- Write formally in the third person: "This examiner," "This assessor," or "The evaluator."
- Capitalize names of tests, subtests and clusters.
- Spell out acronyms for tests in the first usage.
- Use headings to guide the reader through the content.
- Use words that aid in transitions (*Sequencing*: then, next, since; *Cause and Effect*: therefore, consequently, as a result; *Contrast*: however, conversely, nevertheless, although).

Report Writing Don'ts

- Minimize the use of jargon, technical terms and acronyms.
- Avoid colloquialisms.
- Avoid choppy sentences.
- Avoid using a passive voice. Example: A social skills group was recommended for Ben by a therapist. (Written in passive voice). Better: The therapist recommended that Ben join a social skills group. (Active voice).
- Do not use judgmental language: Maria *suffers* from ADHD; Michael has *poor* math skills.

Review Your Rough Draft

Whether you read over your report the same date it is finished or within the next few days, pay careful attention to the content, as well as mechanical errors. "Some people find it useful to wait a day or more before editing, to permit viewing their work more objectively. Sometimes when you read what you have written immediately upon completion, you only see what you intended to communicate" (Lichtenberger et al. 2004: 29). As you are editing and revising your report, evaluate whether it can be easily understood. It can be very helpful to have someone else read and proofread for you. A trusted colleague or partner (even one who is not in the field) can be very helpful in giving feedback about readability and clarity. Of course, any proofreader must be trustworthy and understand confidentiality. Additionally, it is best practice to *redact or remove* all identifying information prior to having someone else proofread your report.

Confidentiality

Placing the word *confidential* in bold at the top of your report may not be adequate, as it is a bit generic. In *Essentials of Assessment Report Writing*, 2nd edition, Schneider and colleagues make some suggestions for creating statements of confidentiality:

- This report contains privileged and confidential information.
- This report contains confidential client information and may not be released without the written permission of the parent or guardian.
- The contents of this report have been shared with the child's parents or guardian. Copies of this report may be released only by the parents.

However, if you have assessed as a staff member for an independent school, this statement may be appropriate: The contents of this report have been shared with the child's parents or guardian. Copies of this report may be released only by the parents and in accordance with the school's policy regarding student records.

(Schneider et al. 2018: 247)

96 *Writing a High-Quality Assessment Report*

Conclusion

Crafting a well-written report is a complex endeavor. It requires thoughtful analysis, strong writing skills, detailed descriptions of the student's strengths and weaknesses, and it must be internally consistent. Use the format most professionals follow and include the required sections. The report should be written to answer the referring questions and keep the student or client in mind. It may contain questions not in the original referral and may include recommendations to refer allied professionals. It serves a different purpose than an IEP. One written with a strengths-based approach can help the student, teachers and parents recognize and leverage strengths. Acknowledgement of a student's interests and affinities may lead to greater self-awareness, self-advocacy and motivation for the student. Since the ultimate goal for conducting an assessment is uncovering and reporting on essential findings, learning to write a compelling and cogent report is a skill worth mastering.

Self-review Questions for Students and Professionals

1 Compare the list of nine items to be included in a formal report against one you have written. Does your report have all of the items? If not, what might you include in future reports?
2 Consider adding a list of questions before you write any report. Who can answer them? Would it be useful to determine the answers before you write the Recommendations?
3 Do you write SMART recommendations?
4 Are some of your recommendations strengths-based? If not, re-write at least one.
5 Evaluate a recent report of yours using the "Writing Dos" and "Writing Don'ts" lists.
6 Why is including a confidentiality statement important?

Questions for Parents

1 Think about the last meeting you attended at your child's school and/or the report you received.

    a How much time at the meeting was devoted to discussing your child's strengths?
    b Can you identify and make a list of your child's strengths and affinities? (Keeping such a list which, you add to over time, can help you gauge your child's progress and resiliency.)
    c Could you share them at a school meeting?

2 Were any of the goals (in an IEP) or recommendations (in the ET's report) strength-based?
3 If not, could you advocate to include them in future meetings and reports?

Resources

AET Code of Ethics: www.aetonline.org/index.php/about/code-of-ethics

Flanagan, D. P., Ortiz, E. O. & Alfonso, V. C. (2013). *Essentials of Cross-Battery Assessment*, 3rd edition. Hoboken, NJ: John Wiley & Sons.

Fuchs L. S. & Fuchs D. (2005). Enhancing Mathematical Problem-Solving for Students with Disabilities. *Journal of Special Education*, 39: 45–57.

Kaufman, A.S. and Lichtenberger, E.O. and Breaux, K. (2005). *Essentials of KABC-III Assessment*. Hoboken, NJ: John Wiley & Sons.

Marshall, M. (2013). Beyond the Scores: Examining the Context and Purpose of Assessment. *The Educational Therapist*, 34(2): 9–25.

Marshall, M. and Matthaei, D. (2015) Sharing Assessment Findings: Writing a High Quality Report. *The Educational Therapist*, 36(1): 7–15.

Motion Math: motionmathgames.com

Quick Math Fact games: multiplication.com

Scaptura, C.Suh, J. and Mahaffey, G. (2007). Using Art to Teach Fractions Decimal and Percent Equivalents. *Math Teaching in the Middle School*, 34(2): 24–28.

Three-Corner Multiplication and Division Flash Cards: www.trendenterprises.com/products/t1671

Wendling, B., and Mather, N. (2008). *Essentials of Evidence-Based Academic Intervention*. Hoboken, NJ: John Wiley & Sons.

References

Bates, J. D. (2000). *Writing with Precision: How to Write so that you Cannot Possibly be Misunderstood*. New York: Penguin Books.

Fuchs L. S. & Fuchs D. (2002). Mathematical Problem-Solving Profiles of Students with Mathematics Disabilities with and Without Comorbid Reading Disabilities. *Journal of Learning Disabilities*, 35: 557–563.

Lichtenberger, E. O. and Breaux, K. (2010). *Essentials of WIAT-3 and KTEA-2 Assessment*. Hoboken, NJ: John Wiley & Sons.

Lichtenberger, E. O., Mather, N. & Kaufman, N. (2004). *Essentials of Assessment Report Writing*. Hoboken, NJ: John Wiley & Sons.

Mather, N. and Jaffe, L. (2016) *Woodcock-Johnson IV: Reports, Recommendations, and Strategies 3rd Edition*. Hoboken, NJ: John Wiley & Sons.

Mazzocco M. M. (2008). Defining and Differentiating Mathematical Learning Disabilities and Difficulties. In D. B. Berch & M. M. Mazzocco (Eds.), *Why Is Math So Hard for Some Children? The Nature and Origins of Mathematical Learning Difficulties and Disabilities*, 29–47. Baltimore, MD: Brookes Publishing Company

McDougall, D. & Brady, M. P. (1998). Initiating and Fading Self-management Interventions to Increase Math Fluency in General Education Classes. *Exceptional Children*, 64(2): 151–166.

McDougall, D., Skouge J., Farrell, C. A. & Hoff, K. (2006). Research on Self-management Techniques Used by Students with Disabilities in General Education Settings: A Promise Fulfilled. *Journal of the American Academy of Special Education Professionals*, 1: 36–73.

Rawe, J. (Undated). Strengths-Based IEPs: What You Need to Know. Retrieved from www.understood.org/en/school-learning/special-services/ieps/strengths-based-ieps-what-you-need-to-know

98 *Writing a High-Quality Assessment Report*

Roth, D. (2005). Public School Ambivalence about the Role of the Private Practitioner in the IEP Process Advice to Educational Therapists from a Director of Special Education. *The Educational Therapist*, 26(2).

Schneider, J. W., Lichtenberger, E. O., Mather, N. & Kaufman, N. (2018). *Essentials of Assessment Report Writing*, 2nd edition. Hoboken, NJ: John Wiley & Sons.

6 How to Orally Present Your Findings

Preparing to Present

Writing the report is an important professional responsibility. Sometimes, graduate students who are becoming ETs will become enamored of the assessment process. While their enthusiasm is wonderful to observe, they ask how long does it take to write an assessment report? Of course, that depends on the number of instruments you administered and the complexity of the referral questions. But, I usually say, "Count the number of hours you spent conducting the assessment. Now double or triple that to score, analyze, and write a cogent report!"

Spending the time analyzing the scores and crafting a well-written report prepares you to *present* your results or essential findings. Sadly, your written report might languish in a file, rarely read, or never be fully appreciated. The oral presentation *may be* the key to establishing the parental (and school) trust in your findings and create the "buy in" needed to generate empathy and establish the desired changes for the student.

Think about the audience to whom you will be presenting and where the meeting will take place. Is it to the parents only? Will the student be present? (Consider the age and grade of the student and the advantages and disadvantages of having the student present.) Are you presenting in your office? Or, are you presenting to the school team as the school-based ET and established member of the staff? Or, will you be presenting to the school team as an "outsider" hired by the family? Where you will be presenting, your role, and how you will be perceived are important factors to consider. Different settings imply distinctive roles. There are useful strategies to ensure your work is well-received. It is best to plan accordingly.

If you are assessing using non-standardized and/or self-created instruments, you communicate the results in the manner that you usually would in the context of establishing baseline skills and setting goals for your work. You would present the results in your office, by phone or email to get confirmation of goals you have set for your work with the student. Of course, it is important to document these goals and re-visit them regularly as a way of documenting progress. This is the ongoing assessment suggested in Chapter 1 of this book

100 *How to Orally Present Your Findings*

and by Dr. Kaganoff in *The Clinical Practice of Educational Therapy: Learning and Functioning with Diversity*: "Many ETs engage in systematic goal setting by the client, and the goals themselves are used to measure progress ... The ongoing job of the ET is to be a careful observer and a trusted witness" (Ficksman and Adelizzi 2018: 270).

Kaganoff also stated that:

> The skilled ET regards all observational data as material that contributes to the initial and ongoing diagnostic process. Each contact with the client will be seen as a step in refining the initial diagnosis that is the basis of the instruction plan, or alternately, in refining or redirecting the intervention plan. The collection of diagnostic data does not stop.
>
> (Kaganoff 2019: 17)

Sharing the results of formal assessment (using standardized assessments) done by the ET for private purposes usually occurs in your office. One of the most important considerations is—will all principal parties be present? Information not expressed to all parties may not ever be actually received by the other parties. Or the information may be mis-stated if "translated" by the other parent who did not fully comprehend the material. And/or that parent may have a biased point of view and choose to express *only part* of the information. I have been in the situation where one parent stated she could not be in the same room as her soon to be ex-husband. Since I firmly believe in having all parties receive the same important information and at the same time, I arranged for a video conference to take place. Another important consideration is the length of time needed for the meeting. You should inform all parties as to the expected duration. If one party were to rush off before the end of the meeting, possible misunderstandings (or incomplete understanding) could ensue. In office meetings where I present assessment findings, I follow the presentation process outlined later in this chapter.

Being a school-based ET (one who is employed by the independent school) is common-place in the San Francisco Bay area (Marshall 2016). This unique role allows one to understand the school's mission, culture, educational approaches and the curricular expectations for each grade level. When one has an established role in the school, a trusted relationship usually follows. Before conducting assessment for the independent school, I elicit referral questions, view work samples, observe the student in the classroom(s), have a completed developmental history, and talk with parents about their perceptions of the student's strengths, affinities and possible academic issues. A consent form is signed by the parent and assessment begins. Upon completion of the assessment, I give a *draft* of the narrative report and *appendix*, which lists all the scores, to the teacher(s) and school administrator in charge of student services (usually the head of school.) Then, I arrange a time to meet to discuss the findings, recommendations, and the implications for services and any proposed accommodations. If the draft report needs revisions, I make them before the

How to Orally Present Your Findings   101

parent meeting. That way, the school presents a united viewpoint to the parents. I do *not* send a report to parents beforehand, as I want to be the professional who initially presents the results and explains what the scores mean, with the goal of coming to a *shared understanding* about the student.

If you have been hired by the family to attend a school-based meeting, attempt to establish a relationship with the school officials, particularly the teacher(s) of the student. Likely, you understand the parents' intent for your presence at the meeting and this may influence the approach you take in reaching out to school personnel. One important thing to ascertain is whether this is a regularly scheduled school meeting such as parent conference. If that is the case, conferences are typically scheduled for short periods of time, such as twenty minutes. All you can do in that meeting is establish your role with the student and listen to the teacher(s) report on the student's current level of functioning. Simply stated, there will not be time for you to meaningfully present any assessment results. A better plan is to request a *separate*, subsequent and lengthier meeting time to present the results. It is quite important to reach out to the teacher(s) prior to the meeting to discuss the key findings and what you intend to present to gauge any reactions. In Cassie's case, creating a rapport and a willingness by her math teacher to engage in ongoing and regular collaboration was essential. Understanding his homework policies and exploring the possibilities for altering Cassie's homework load on the days where she would be spending an hour after school to work on math was vital. It was critical that he understand that Cassie might to do a bit of her math homework in a session but the ET's primary role would be to carefully "back fill" all of the 3rd-5th grade skills she was missing.

Very early in my career as an ET, I was asked by the parents to attend a meeting they had requested with the teacher. "Katie" was in the 2nd grade and I had been her ET for 2 months. She was an "emerging" reader who had recently demonstrated good progress in her decoding skills and was now reading, at home, without being asked to do so. Her parents were very pleased and relieved. I had not ascertained that the parents had set the agenda for the meeting and I had failed to have a conversation with the teacher prior to the meeting. The parents asked the teacher his evaluation of "Katie's" reading skills. They were primed to hear positive comments and were stunned when he said sadly, "She is by far the lowest reader in the class." They looked at him in disbelief and me in dismay. Whom should they trust? They should believe the teacher's view—right? They wanted to rely on me. They looked back and forth between us in confusion. I thought deeply for a minute and said, "Maybe we are both correct." Having done a recent progress update, I could readily state details about the types of phonic patterns she could read now. I was able to express the level of book she was now reading independently in my office and the parents were able to rally and assert that Katie was reading at night "for fun." Now, the teacher was stunned. That day I learned several hallmark truths. First, I should have talked with the teacher before the conference. Secondly, a student may demonstrate significant gains in your office, well

102 *How to Orally Present Your Findings*

before s/he may demonstrate them at home or at school. It does not mean the gains are not valid; they have not generalized to home or school *yet*.

The need for respectful collaboration with school partners is stated by several authors in the edited volume *The Clinical Practice of Educational Therapy: Learning and Functioning with Diversity* (Ficksman and Adelizzi 2018). Kass states that although ETs may view themselves as an expert:

> the ET must take into account the context of the classroom, the training and attitude of the classroom teacher, and the knowledge base of the school administration when proposing curriculum and behavioral accommodations … She must take care not to come across as the "expert" who knows the best way to help the challenged learner become successful! In all collaboration, the ET must maintain an attitude of respect for the professional knowledge of the classroom teacher, administrator, and allied professional …
>
> (Ficksman and Adelizzi 2018: 43)

My view is that the ET has a wonderful opportunity by working one-on-one with the student. However, she does not have the *daily* experience of working with the student *in the context of the classroom and school setting*. Kass adds that it is always best to demonstrate "humility, openness to hearing other perspectives, and an appreciation of the expertise of the other professionals" (ibid.) when collaborating with school personnel.

Dr. Kass also stated that many school professionals "are ambivalent concerning collaboration with private practitioners" (Ficksman and Adelizzi 2018: 44). This may be due to some ET's lack of appreciation for the *differences* between what is possible when working one-on-one with the student and what is feasible in the school's setting. In Chapter 5, remember the discussion of the school's "deficiency" model as opposed to a strength-based one. This can affect their viewpoint.

Clearly, it is essential to prepare for each different type of meeting. It is essential to determine your *specific goals* for the oral presentation. For example, I had been asked by the school, where I was employed as the ET, to uncover why "Sam," a highly verbal 4th grader, wrote so little. Almost nothing was written during the daily twenty minutes of "journal time" his teacher complained. The parents said Sam balked at doing homework which required *any* writing! Their question was-why was Sam so recalcitrant and uncooperative about writing? You know that assessment should answer important questions. Through the assessment process and, in discussing with Sam his experience of writing, I had the answers to those questions. However, I had generated another *specific goal* for the meeting which was to *add to* the previous question. I sought to *change their perceptions* regarding Sam's writing.

I wanted others to understand that Sam was not purposely under-performing but presently was unable to think about what to write, hold his pencil efficiently, remember how to form letters, spell, focus on the mechanics of writing and vary his sentence structure, all at the same time, as most other 4th graders could. The assessment results demonstrated that he could do many of those skills in isolation. Sam told me he had very "listy writing." He was keenly aware that he wrote like he was "making a shopping list," because by not varying the sentence structure he could write more. Isn't that what his teacher wanted? And, he was cognizant that his father often criticized his handwriting as being "too messy." That, too, impeded his ability to complete some of his homework for fear of his father's recrimination. Actually, if one considered Sam's approach to doing his homework, he was happy to read and to do math calculations. My goal was to create greater empathy for Sam and have the others understand that his writing skills *were* developing but he could not, yet, write for long periods of time due to visual motor integration issues. The twenty-minute "journal writing time" was too long and "was a nightmare" according to Sam. The recommendations would feature ways for Sam to create journal entries or stories by using a voice to text option, storyboarding, or dictating to an adult, after which he only carefully copied one or two sentences from his journal until his fine motor skills improved. Sam *wanted* to write well.

Beginning the Meeting

I begin a presentation meeting by acknowledging the importance of sharing the results together and working towards a common understanding of the strengths and issues. I start by asking if the student expressed any feelings about assessment experience. The feedback is always affirmative. "He said he had fun! How is that even possible?" exclaims the mother. I ask this question to underscore that the results are likely accurate since it was a positive experience. Most parents reflect back on taking a "high stakes test" such a final exam or as the Scholastic Achievement Test (SAT), Graduate Record Exam (GRE), Law Bar Exam, or Medical College Admission Test (MCAT). They recall such tests as being pressure-packed. I explain to the parents that the type of assessment the student just undertook is a *relational process*. It has an easy going "give and take" quality where the examiner watches the student's level of concentration and works to assist the student in maintaining her focus and attention to the task. Making eye contact, praising effort and often using the student's name can serve to establish rapport and cue concentration—"Lindsey, try this next one." "Sam, look here," as you point to the next item. In this type of assessment, administration is stopped if the student appears unduly fatigued or seems unusually distracted.

I also explain to the parent(s) that this type of testing is *very different* from what the student experiences every day at school because the assessment begins where the student can do the work easily (the basal) and each subtest or test ends when the child cannot do the work (the ceiling). There are no lingering points of confusion or long periods of frustration as may occur often in the school setting. This assessment process is generally comfortable and agreeable. In addition, each student has the full attention of a kind adult which is also usually enjoyable.

104 *How to Orally Present Your Findings*

Remind the parents (and other participants) what the referring questions were. Know what are the key findings, which are the points you want to emphasize. Do not read from a report as you should maintain eye contact to watch for parental reactions. Be keenly aware that each parent may be receiving the information differently and be ready to gently ask follow-up questions. I state that there is a written report which will be shared but I want to talk through and explain the results *before* giving out a copy of the report to each person present. If you read a report or visually refer to it too often, likely you will lose track of important interactions and reactions. Practice so the points you wish to emphasize flow well and you are comfortable talking about them.

Next, I acknowledge that we all know the student in different ways: The parents know the student holistically, the student's development and temperament and across time. The teacher (s) know the student within the context of years of experience (usually) and in comparison, to scores of grade-level peers. I stress that I know the student the least, and from the context of norms which are established among a large number of same-aged peers and from having assessed many students. I explain that I will stop at intervals to ask the question, "Does this sound like I am describing 'Lindsey' or 'Sam'"? I ask for honest reactions saying that, if does not sound like your child or that student in their class, it will be important to discuss what does not seem accurate. If you omit this important step, stakeholders may dismiss the remainder of the findings if some aspects seem false to them.

As stated in Chapter 4, I make certain to quote the student throughout the assessment results. The student's actual experience of the strengths and struggles are key to validating the test results and assists in keeping the focus on the student (see Figure 4.2). Parents may not fully believe test scores but they will usually heed the anguished comments of their child, "I can't read this! It makes my head hurt just to look at all these words!" "Only smart kids can think of something to write during journal time." "Oh no—not algebra problems. I get a stomach ache every day knowing that I am walking into my algebra class."

Presenting the Results Visually

Rather than a wholly oral presentation, I prepare and present the key scores on a 11" × 17" sheet of paper. This reference guides my comments and gives those in attendance a visual reference in addition to my verbal descriptions. Many tests currently published have the capability to print out a graphic of the scores. Guard against this as your sole means of understanding the test results. This is simply too easy and too mechanical. It does not allow the assessor to *grapple* with understanding the *relationship* and *meaning* of each score, *between* scores, and *between* different tests. I use color coding to link and distinguish between different tests and subtests results (see Figure 6.1).

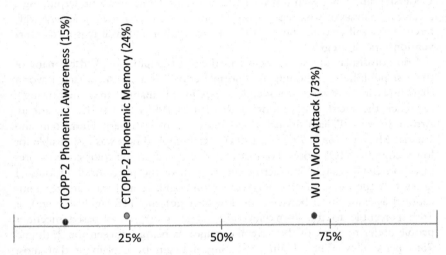

Figure 6.1 Horizontal Scale Scores (Sample)

106 *How to Orally Present Your Findings*

For example, after conducting a reading assessment, all the assessment related to decoding skills might be in purple; reading fluency might be marked in green, while those that measure reading accuracy in blue and scores measuring reading comprehension might be in black. Because the underpinning of developing decoding in reading is related to phonemic awareness, those scores would also be marked in purple to emphasize and underscore their relationship. And, if reading decoding skills are low, and so are the phonemic awareness scores, that signals a need to train and develop phonemic awareness skills in order to support decoding skills. However, if a student's vocabulary is strong, reading decoding skills are average or better and recognition of high frequency words are adequate but reading comprehension is weak, the finding is the need to train and develop reading fluency. Understanding what each test measures, each academic area's underpinnings, a careful analysis of what each score means and the *relationship between* different tests will lead to the creation of meaningful and well-reasoned interventions and strategies.

I do not display or use the bell-shaped curved graphic supplied by many of the test publishers. Although the "normal curve" is a statistical fact, I worry that displaying a student's academic scores in this manner may unknowingly reference the racist publications in the 1960s–1990s of Charles Spearman, Arthur Jensen, William Shockley and more recently Richard Herrnstein and Charles Murray (*The Bell Curve*, 1994), which implied race was responsible for lower cognitive (IQ) scores. For many years, I displayed the color-coded scores in a horizontal straight line across the bottom of the page. And, although I know that the range of "average scores" on cognitive and standardized educational assessments is between 85 (low average) and 115 (high average) or 16th percentile to the 84th percentile range, most school-based meetings people prefer to think of the "average range" as being between the 25th and 75th percentiles. When I am presenting, I begin by explaining that most people think of "average" as 50% (or 100 Standard Score) and draw a thin pencil line there. Then, I mark the 25th and 75th percentiles saying, "We will be paying attention to the scores that represent strengths (or relative strengths for that student) because we will want to harness them to work on areas of weakness."

More recently, I create the graphic *in the vertical* with higher scores at the top and lower ones at the bottom (see Figure 6.2). I still draw a pencil line at 50th percentile and mark the 25th and 75th percentiles, saying, "In the report you will read descriptors like 'high average' or 'low average' and this graphic will help you understand these terms better." Displaying the student's scores vertically does not bring to mind the bell-shaped curve. Instead, the vertical representation looks more like a temperature thermometer and relative highs and lows are more easily recognized by parents and teachers. This graphic representation readily guides the discussion into the summary and recommendations.

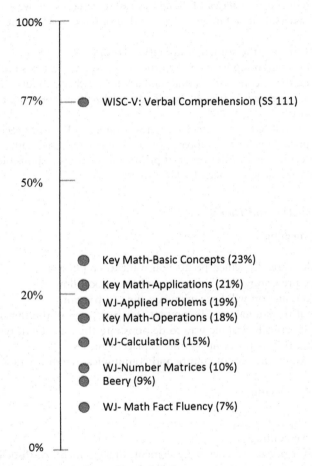

Figure 6.2 Cassie's Scores Vertical Scale

108 *How to Orally Present Your Findings*

The Summary and Recommendations

As clusters of lower scores denote areas of weakness, I consciously remind the listeners of the initial referral question(s) and link these patterns to the findings. These moments of clarity are "bittersweet" for the parents. As you may recall, I know from personal experience that it is very hard to have your child seemingly reduced to a series of "cold" assessment scores. Strive to make the process of assessment a bit less harsh and more focused on the individual student.

Remind others of the student's strengths. Towards the end of the meeting, I hand out the written report turned to the page containing the summary paragraph. I state that I consider it a draft and ask for feedback about anything that is unclear or needs correcting so that I can finalize the report after they take the full report home and read it.

Reading a well-written summary creates a direct link to the recommendations and presents a clear rationale for adopting each one. Once you have reached agreement about the order of priority and who is responsible for each, agree upon on a time to check back to assess progress.

Presentation Dos and Don'ts

Before the meeting:

- Consider carefully which points you want to emphasize.
- Practice presenting the findings to ensure a good flow.
- Make certain you will have adequate time to present.
- Decide if the student will be present (for part or all of the time).
- Prepare a visually graphic way to demonstrate the assessment results.
- Consider the room set up, furniture placement, etc.
- Get to know the school culture and communicate with teachers.

During the meeting:

- Listen respectfully to others.
- Make eye contract.
- Watch for nonverbal cues of agreement, disagreement, or disbelief.
- Pause to invite questions or elicit reactions.
- Ask: "Does this sound like I am describing your child/the student?"
- Quote the student when appropriate.
- Use understandable language.
- Define essential terms.
- Compliment the teacher(s) on their contributions in helping others to understand the student.
- Work to create a shared understanding. If there are disagreements, note that and suggest ways for a resolution (over time, if necessary).

How to Orally Present Your Findings 109

At the end of the meeting:

- Ask if the recommendations are reasonable and possible.
- Review who is responsible for implementing each recommendation.
- Determine a reasonable time to meet again or talk to gauge progress.
- End by thanking attendees for their time, interest in the student, and thoughtful input.

Do *not*:

- Read from your report.
- Use educational jargon.
- Exclude others from speaking by dominating the conversation.
- Exceed the amount of time allotted for the meeting.
- Position yourself as the "sole expert" on the student, as it will not produce the desired collaboration.
- Forget that what is possible in your office may *not* be possible in a classroom.
- Attempt to impose your recommendations on others.

Through the whole assessment process (which includes this meeting) comes acknowledgment that the student *is* struggling. But, now there is a shared understanding for *why*. Once these reason(s) are well-defined, a path for specific, individualized, research-based interventions can become clear. This chapter was designed to share some guiding principles for presenting your assessment results to others. Each of you has (or will develop) a professional communication style. You do not have to replicate my approach *exactly* to be successful.

Always remember, the reason for conducting an assessment is to answer important questions. If you have achieved clarity about the student's strengths and areas of need, your work can create hope and a way forward.

Conclusion

In conclusion, this may be an unusual textbook as I have endeavored to encapsulate my experiences with assessment over the past forty years, having assessed hundreds of students and leading well over six hundred meetings (a rough estimate) sharing those assessment results privately, and in both public and independent school settings. In this book, I have shared much of my life's professional work and experiences. Dr. Ann Kaganoff wrote in her book, *Best Practices in Educational Therapy*:

> Each of us, new and the veteran has a special responsibility to the profession, to be sure that all of our best practices are recorded and made available to the wider world, where there is such a great need for what we do.
> (Kaganoff 2019: 248)

110   *How to Orally Present Your Findings*

In this book, I have made that attempt and tried to guide you, lead you and sometimes spur you into thinking more broadly and deeply about your assessment practices. I sincerely hope you have had many of your approaches validated. More importantly, I hope you will become more nuanced in how you approach assessment, how you write reports, and how you share your findings with the student, parents and educators, after having read this book.

Finally, these are my key findings regarding Cassie and how I would explain them to her:

> Cassie, you have many verbal strengths which can support getting better at math. You have good logical reasoning skills and that is a hard skill to learn—so that is great! You are spirited and stubborn and I think admirable those characteristics in a young woman. But this is the year to get comfortable with math. Cassie, you do not have a specific reason why you can't learn math—but your math skills are quite behind others in your grade. I sense you know that.
>
> It is sometimes hard to learn new things and *especially hard* to learn things we aren't interested in or don't like. It's time to actually learn all of those math facts. You will need them going forward and will be quite stuck without learning them. There are 144 multiplication math facts. Did you see that when you colored all the math facts you *do* know on the math fact chart, you know all but 32 of them? And once you learn "facts" like 7 × 8 = 56, you will also know 8 × 7 = 56 so you can color in two spaces at once! And when you know 7 × 8, you will know 56 ÷ by 8 = 7. Numbers are made up of patterns and I will help you discover them.
>
> You are going to need to write down more of your calculations when math problems get more complicated. You take notes from when you read. So, think about why you do that and how writing down notes helps you. It's like that in math, too.
>
> Math is all around you and useful in many daily activities. Let's find which ones you enjoy doing the most. I hope we can be partners. Now, are you ready to get to work?

Self-review Questions for Students and Professionals

1 Think about a recent time when you presented assessment results orally. Compare the dos/don't lists to how you prepare. Is there anything you might change in your preparation?
2 Do you prepare differently for different types of meetings? If so, how? Why?
3 Think about a recent time when you presented assessment results orally. Compare the list of dos/don'ts to how you present. Is there anything you might change in your approach to presenting?
4 Do you use a visual representation of the scores when presenting? If so, have you gotten feedback as to its helpfulness? If not, would you consider using one now?

5 Do you think that all parents should receive the initial assessment results at the same time? If so, what techniques do you employ to achieve this?
6 A parent asks to record the meeting so the parent/partner who cannot be present can hear it. How do you respond?

Questions for Parents

1 Think about the last meeting you attended where assessment results were discussed. Did you understand the results? If not, what could you do differently?
2 How do *you* prepare to attend a meeting where assessment results will be discussed?
3 How often do you attend by yourself? How hard is it to accurately convey the results to your spouse/partner? What could be done differently?
4 At the last meeting did you receive a visual representation of the scores? If not, would that have helped you understand them better?

References

Ficksman, M. and Adelizzi, J. (Eds.). (2018). *The Clinical Practice of Educational Therapy: Learning and Functioning with Diversity*. New York: Routledge.
Kaganoff, A. (2019). *Best Practices in Educational Therapy*. New York: Routledge.
Marshall, M. (2016). The School-Based Educational Therapist. *The Educational Therapist*, 37: 2.

Index

accommodations 2, 82, 83, 88, 90, 100, 102

age-equivalent scoring 6, 15, 17, 18, 19, 22, 25, 27, 30, 31, 50, 60, 61

American Educational Research Association (AERA) 11, 42

American Psychological Association (APA) 11,35 50, 80

assessment battery 6, 14, 65, *66, 91*

assessment plan 64, 65, 67

Association of Educational Therapists (AET) 10, 11, 12, 35

attention 4, 64, 65, 73, 77

    ADHD 41, 42, 95

    sustained attention 4, 67, 73

auditory discrimination 65

auditory memory 31, **44**, 74

auditory perceptual 36

auditory processing 31, 32

background knowledge 32, 65, 67, 71, 72

basal 48, 59, 103

Beery Test of Visual-Motor Integration 29, 37, **44**, 67, 78, 79, 84, *107*

bell-shaped/normal curve 17, 52, *53*, 106

bullet points 89, 94

Buros Mental Measurement Yearbook (see MMY)

capitalization 67

cascade of events 46, *47*

chronological age 46, 48, 55

cloze procedure 32, 33, 72

code of ethics 10–12, 42, 82, 97

collaboration 11, 101, 102, 109

Common Core (math) 42, 79, 84

computer-generated scoring 48, 91, 94

confidence intervals 57, *58*, 60

confidence level 46, 57

confidentiality 95, 96

constellations/constellations approach 62, 65, 67, 77

Council for Exceptional Children 10, 42

criterion-referenced tests 7, 9, 20, 49, 50, 68, 69

cross-cultural fairness 15, 16

CTOPP-2 29, 30, **39**, **44**, 105

derived scores 5, 46, 48, 52, 55, 57, **74**, 75

developmental constructs 63

diagnostic 12, 21, 22, 24, 25, 26, **39–41**, 79, 100

    tasks 8

    teaching 68

    tests 7, 24, **39**, **41–42**, 69

Decoding (reading) 20, **38–39**, 72, 101, 106

discrepancy formula/model 2, 52, 82

domino effect 47

ecology of assessment 73

error analysis 5, 8, 18, 84

ethics 3, 9–13, 15, 16, 35, 82

examiner's/technical manual 11, 19, 30, 32, 36, 37, **40**, **44**, 55, 56, 59

executive function 67

expository text 33, 34, 65, 71

Ficksman, M. and Adelizzi, J. 100, 102, 111

Findings 3, 4, 15, 46, 47, 79, 82, 83, 85, 86, 87, 88, 89, 90, 94, 99, 100, 104, 108, 110

Fuchs, L. and Fuchs, D. 79, 93, 97

GORT-5 16, 17, 33, 34, 35, 37, **38**, 71, 72, 73, 79, 80
grade-equivalents 17, 19, 21, 25, 31, 32, 36, 37, 50, 61
grammar 33, 65, 67, 72, 94

handwriting 67, 103
hearing 52, 56, 61, 65, 84
hypothesis/ working hypothesis testing 1, 5, 62, 64–69, 71, 73, 74, 75, 79

IDEA 17, 20, 52, 61
Individual Educational Plan (IEP) 1, 3, **38**, **78**
informal measures/informal assessments 3, 7, 10, 13, 27, 68
informed consent 14
International Reading Association 50
intervention(s) 15, 17, 18, 20, 23, 26, 27, **40**, 83, 85, 88, 90, 91, 97, 106, 109
item analysis 15, 77

Kaganoff, A. 8, 9, 100, 109, 111
Keukrug, E. and Fawcett, R. 16, 37, 80
Key Math-3 25, 36, **42**, 57, 60, 67, 75, 76, 77, 78, 79, 107
KTEA-3 9, 17, 18, **38**, **40**, **42**, 97

language 4, 5, 6, 10, 22, 23, 24, 31, 34, 36, **40**, **44**, 65, 67, 68, 71, 72, 74, 80
  expressive 67
  load 73, 74
  oral 17, 22, 24, **39–40**
  receptive 67
  written 17, 18, 21, 22, 23–25, 36, **39–40**, 67, 85, 89
learning profile 2, 33, 74, 83

Mazzocco, M. 93, 97
Marshall, M. 9, 97, 100, 111
Marshall, M. and Matthaei, D. 8, 9, 13, 14, 36, 79, 97
math calculation(s) 28, 78, 85, 103
math fact fluency 28, 51, 60, **76**, 77, **78**, 79, 83, 92, 97, 107, 110
Mather, N. 5, 9, 61, 90
Mather, N. and Wendling, B. 9, 79, 97
mean 49–52, *54*, 55, 59
MMY 13, 15–22, 23, 24, 25, 26–28, 29–31, 35, 49, 56, 59, 61, 88

National Council on Measurement in Education 11, 35, 50
Nelson-Denny Reading Test (NDRT) 18, **38**
non-standardized assessment/measures 6, 67, 68, 79, 99
normal distribution 50, 51, 52, *54*, 61
number facts 27, 67
number sense 67, 93

oral directions **44**, 74
orthographic knowledge 67

PAL II 18, 19, **38**, **40**
PAL II-M 26, **42**
parallel forms 16, 22, **38–44**, 56
passage comprehension 22, 32, 34, 35, **39**, 72
patterns of strengths and weaknesses 5, 15, 20, 24, 87
pencil grasp/grip 29, 67
percentile rank(s) 6, 15, 22, 23, 25, 27, 28 30, 34, **49**, 50, 51, 55, 56, 59, 60, 63, 69, 72, **76**, 78, 84
phonological processing 29, 30, 31, 35, **38**, **44**, 63
Practicality 16
Presentation Do's 108
Presentation Dont's 108
problem solving 2, 4, 28, **43**, 74, **78**, 79, 84, 85, 97
professional voice 15, 81, 88
psychometrics 45, 55
punctuation 5, 67, 94

RAN/RAS tests 30, 31, 35, **44**
raw score 46–48, 51, 57, 59
reading 3–7, 13, 16–22, 25, 27, 28, 30–37, **38–39**, 45, 50, 56, 61, 63–65, 68, 69, 71, 72, 74, **78**, 79, 80, 89, 90, 91, 97, 101, 106
  accuracy 33, 72, 73, 106
  comprehension 20, 32–34, **39**, 65, 72, 73, 106
  fluency 20, 22, 30, **38**, **39**, 72, 90, 96
  rate 17, 33, **38**
recommendations 1, 3, 15, 46, 48, 79, 81–92, 94, 96, 97, 100, 103, 106, 108, 109
reliability 10, 13, 15–20, 24, 27, 29, 32, **49**, 56–57
report of Findings 15, 47, 85
report Writing Do's 94

114 *Index*

report Writing Dont's 95
rubrics 68–70

scaled scores 19, 26, 28, 30, 31, 34, 49
Schneider, J., et. al. 9, 51, 57, 61, 65,
  80, 90, 95
Scholastic Aptitude Test (SAT) 52, *54,*
  55, 103
school-based Educational Therapist
  99, 100
scientific method 65
self-regulation 64
Shrank, F. and Flanagan, D.
  72, 75, 80
SMART goals 90, 91, 95
spatial 74, 77
Specific Learning Disability (SLD)
  2, 20, 61
speech language pathologist 10, 52, 61
spelling 4, 7, 21, 25, **40–41**, 67, 94
standard deviation(SD) 23, 25, **49,**
  51–52, 55
Standard Error of Measurement(SEM)
  15, 56, 57, *58,* 60
standard scores (SS) 15, 16, 19, 21, 23,
  25, 27, 31, 45, **49,** 50–52, 55, 57,
  59–60, 86, *107*
standardized assessment(s) 9, 14, 15, 30,
  36, **49,** 50, 60, 69, 79
Standards for Educational and
  Psychological Testing 11, 35
standards-based assessment 7, 69
strengths-based report 79, 81, 86
syntax 32, 65, 67, 72

TAPS-4 31, **44**
task analysis 5, 8, 83, 84
technical manual(see examiner's manual)
TEMA-3 27, **42**
test construction 15, 32, 72, 74

test format 16, 32, 62, 72, 73
test protocol 47
test re-test relationship 15,
  16, 56, 57
testing bias 15
TILLS 23, 33, **40**
TOMA-3 27, 28, **42**
TOWL-4 23, 24, 36, **40**
TOWRE-2 19, **38**

validity 10, 13, 15–19, 23, 24, 27,
  29, 32, **49,** 73
vision/visual 71, 74, **78,** 87
  acuity 65, 71
  binocular vision 65, 71
  memory 63, 67
  motor integration 29, 37, **44,** 63,
    67, 73, 75, **78,** 79, 84, 86, 89,
    92, 93, 103
  perception 29
  perceptual skills 89
  spatial 65, 67, 73

Weiss, L. 60
WIAT III 9, 11, 12, 14, 20, 24, 28,
  32, 37, **39, 41, 43,** 48, 52, 61, 62,
  72, 80, 97
WJ IV Ach 9, 11, 12, 21, 22,
  25, 28, 32, 34, 35, **38–39,**
  41–43, 45, 51–52, 57, 60,
  72, 75, **76,** 77, **78,** 79–80,
  85, *105, 107*
working memory 5, 67, 69,
  73, 77, 83
WRAT-5 21, **39, 41, 43**
Wright, P. and Darr Wright
  (Wright's Law), P. 35, 51,
  55, 60, 61

z scores 55